WHEN GOD REIGNS

COVENANT
PUBLISHING

WHEN GOD REIGNS

A Study in the Parables of Jesus

C. Michael Moss

www.covenantpublishing.com

COVENANT
P U B L I S H I N G

Covenant Publishing
P.O. Box 390 Webb City, Missouri 64870
Call toll free at 877.673.1015

Library of Congress Cataloging-in-Publication Data
Moss, C. Michael (Carl Michael), 1950-
    When God reigns : a study in the parables of Jesus / C. Michael Moss.
    p. cm.
    Includes bibliographical references (p. 156) and index.
    ISBN 1-892435-31-4 (pbk.)
    1. Jesus Christ—Parables. I. Title.
    BT375.3.M67 2004
    226.8'06—dc22
                              2004000979

DEDICATION

Dedicated to Carl and Mabel Moss, my parents,
who have always encouraged me
in both ministry and scholarship.

TABLE OF CONTENTS

PREFACE

When Jesus taught those who gathered around Him, He frequently used parables. When He wanted them to understand what their community and their lives would be like if God were to reign, He turned to parables. Parables provide a window into both the mind of Christ and His vision for His people.

This book aims to help the modern reader understand Jesus' message by giving clues as to how one might read the parables of Jesus intelligently. The goal is to assist the student in hearing the parable as those in Jesus' audience would have heard it. The author hopes to assist the student of the parables in developing the heart Jesus seeks so that "he who has ears to hear" might indeed "hear" what Jesus has to say.

CHAPTER 1
When God Reigns

My interest in studying Jesus' parables goes back nearly twenty years. I traveled to my home congregation to witness a Wednesday evening Bible class on the parables that raised my level of frustration with adult Bible classes in local churches. The teacher was leading a discussion of a parable and writing notes on one of those large green chalkboards with knobs on both sides. The teacher said, "Let's see how many lessons we can get from this parable." He began with one column, then another, flipped the chalkboard, and made two more columns. I was able to hold my tongue, but on the way home poured out my frustration to my wife. "A parable cannot mean just anything. It has to have a message." My wife responded, "What are you going to do about it?" That marked the beginning of a collection of books on the parables of Jesus and serious study of the interpretation of the parables.

DEFINITIONS

Perhaps you have heard the definition often given for a parable in Bible classes: "A parable is an earthly story with a heavenly meaning." That definition is a bit too simplistic. The Greek word for parable is *parabolē*. It means literally "to throw alongside." An illustration is thrown alongside a lesson to drive home the point.

The Hebrew/Aramaic word used for a parable is *mashal,* a word for any figure of speech. That word appears thirty-three times in the Old Testament. On twenty-eight instances it is rendered *parabolē* (parable) in the Septuagint, the Greek translation of the Old Testament. The word can refer to proverbs, maxims, similes, allegories, fables, comparisons, riddles, taunts, or stories embodying some truth (Num. 23:7, 18; 1 Sam. 10:12; 24:13; Job 27:1; Ps. 49:4; 78:2; Prov. 1:6; Eccl. 12:9; Isa. 14:4; Ezek. 12:2; 17:2; 24:3; 13; Micah 2:4; Hab. 2:6). Because the Greek word *parabolē* is consistently used to translate that Hebrew/Aramaic word in the New Testament, it at times comes close to duplicating this range of meanings. It can refer to a proverb (Luke 4:23); a profound or obscure saying (Matt. 13:35); a symbol or image that may even be nonverbal (Heb. 9:9; 11:19); or a comparison used to illustrate a point, whether without the form of a story (Matt. 15:15; 24:32) or with the true "parable" (e.g., 13:3-9). Classically a parable is a story used as an illustration. In some way, the story illustrates the point the author or speaker has in mind.

Jesus did not invent the parable. Perhaps the most famous of the Old Testament parables is the parable Nathan the prophet told David after his affair with Bathsheba (2 Sam. 12:1-14).

In Greco-Roman literature the genre "parable" is used in a fairly restricted way. In his *Rhetoric* (2.20) Aristotle discussed two types of proof used in rhetoric. The first is the example (*paradeigma*), which is to be used inductively. The example was then divided into two classes: history and fiction. The fictional examples are again divided into two subclasses: the fable (*logos*) and the comparison (*parabolē*). Fables are impossible or unrealistic fictions. They have animals speaking, and portray events that could never happen. Parables, on the other had, are possible or realistic fiction. The second type of proof is the saying, which is to be used deductively. Again there are two classes: the maxim and the proverb.

The parables in Matthew typically begin with the phrase "the kingdom of heaven is like. . . ." It is imperative to get an idea of what Jesus had in mind when He used the word "kingdom" before one can begin a study of the parables.

Growing up, I remember being taught that there was one phrase in the Lord's prayer that the believer could not pray today, "Thy kingdom come." The kingdom was the church and, therefore, had already come. One should change that line to "Thy kingdom has come." In the prayer itself, there is a clue that this is likely not the case. It is my assumption that the Lord's prayer is poetry. Hebrew poetry is composed of synonymous parallelism. This would make sense of the difference in this prayer between Matthew and Luke. Luke omits two phrases: "Thy will be done" and "but deliver us from evil." They would be the second line which repeats or clarifies the first line in a poem. "Thy kingdom come" would then be equivalent to "Thy will be done." "Lead us not into temptation" is the flip side of "but deliver us from evil."

The Greek and Hebrew words for kingdom emphasize not the realm over which the king exercises his control but the **reign** of the king. For that reason I have entitled this study "When God Reigns." Jesus is informing His listeners that "when God reigns people will live like this. . . ."

The word "kingdom" is used in three different ways in the New Testament. 1) It is sometimes used of the reign of God in the individual's life. A good illustration of this point is seen in Luke 17:21. When asked, "When will your kingdom come?" Jesus responds "the kingdom of God is within you" or "among you" or "in your midst." You are looking for an earthly kingdom, but my kingdom is in your hearts. 2) A second way the word is used can be seen in Matthew 16:18,19. After Peter's great confession, Jesus says, "Upon this rock I will build My church. I will give you the keys to the kingdom." The word "kingdom" can be used of the corporate reign of God in His church. 3) The word "kingdom" can also be used of the final, complete reign of God in heaven. This is a favorite usage for Paul, but it can also be seen in the Gospels. In Mark 14:25, Jesus, after using the cup in instituting the Lord's Supper, says, "Truly I say to you, I will never again drink of the fruit of the vine until that day when I drink it new in the kingdom of God." Jesus is not referring to the first Sunday after Pentecost, but to the grand feast of redemption in heaven at the end time.

The kingdom can then refer to 1) God's reign in the individual's life, 2) His corporate reign in the church, or 3) His final, ultimate reign over all in heaven. One must from the context determine what Jesus or the author has in mind. It can rightly be said, "The kingdom is not the church, but the church is the kingdom."

FEATURES OF THE GOSPELS

It is important to note certain unique features of the Gospels that will affect our interpretation of them.

1. *Jesus Himself wrote nothing.* That is particularly significant. He does not write down what He was saying or write what He wished for us to hear. He was simply speaking to and dealing with people in His day.
2. *We have four Gospels.* It is interesting that some within the early church worked to produce a single Gospel out of all of those Gospels, for example, Tatian's work the *Diatessaron.* Despite those efforts, what survived for us are four independent Gospels.
3. *The Gospels often agree, sometimes verbatim.*
4. *Sometimes they differ, frequently in drastic ways.*
5. *Three are more alike (they are called the Synoptics). One (John's Gospel) is not at all like the other three in events recorded, emphasis, order, vocabulary, etc.*
6. *When one reads a Gospel, he or she is reading a special kind of literature.*

Normally those who study literature talk about different genres or types of literature. A gospel is not like a letter. Just as one would read the newspaper differently from the way he or she would read a book of poetry, one should not expect to read a gospel the same way he/she would read an epistle.

Both epistles and gospels are theological documents. Most readers readily admit that epistles are theological documents written to address ethical and theological issues. We may, however, be tempted to see the Gospels as biographies, and fail to recognize that gospels were also written to deal with theological and ethical problems. Gospels, like epistles, address particular churches with particular problems; however, these two kinds of documents, epistles and gospels, do theology differently. An epistle is a letter that has certain instructions for those who receive it. On the other hand, a gospel provides the reader with a narrative, and from that narrative the reader learns the theology.

7. *When one studies the gospel, he/she is dealing with additional layers that make the study of a Gospel different from interpreting other biblical literature, e.g., epistles.*

Reading a Gospel is a lot different from reading an epistle. If I study 1 Corinthians, I begin with what God through Paul was saying to the church at Corinth. The book wasn't written to me so I must start with Paul and the church at Corinth in AD 52. Only then can I learn God's message for me today.

When one comes to the Gospels, yet another layer is added. First, we have what Jesus was saying to His audience—His disciples, the crowds, the Pharisees, the religious leaders of His day. Jesus Himself, however, wrote nothing. The evangelists recorded what Jesus said and did. They did not, however, simply tell the stories so we would have a record. They chose words that spoke to their audiences. The second level is then what Luke was saying to Theophilus and the church in Asia Minor. They were not confronted with Pharisees and Jewish religious leaders. But what Jesus said to His audience spoke to them. Only after learning what Jesus meant, and what Luke intended for his audience to learn, can we move to ask, "What is God saying to me today?"

HISTORY OF INTERPRETING THE PARABLES

The interpretation of Jesus' parables has a long and winding history. The evangelists themselves took what Jesus said, interpreted it, and applied it to their audiences.

By the second and third century, the method of interpreting the parables changed. Parables were seen as allegories, not as allegorical in manner, but as allegories that needed fanciful and imaginative interpretation.

The allegory provided as an illustration of this method is, in reality, a combination of the allegorical interpretation of the parable of the Good Samaritan by Origen, Augustine, and Jerome. Putting together the interpretation of these three church fathers produces an outlandish interpretation but helps the reader to see the nature of an allegorical interpretation of the parables. In such an allegory, everything stands for something. Every event, every element stands for something in the story. For the early church fathers there was no single, right interpretation.

The story of the Good Samaritan is one students of the Bible know very well. There is a man on a journey. He is met by robbers while on his way from Jerusalem to Jericho. The robbers beat him up and leave him half-dead on the road. Along comes the priest, and he passes by on the other side; then a Levite and he also passes by. Then along comes a Samaritan. He stops and bandages the man's wounds and puts oil and wine on them. He puts the man on his donkey, takes him to the inn, and then says to the innkeeper, "Here are two denarii. Take care of this man, and, if he owes more, I'll pay it when I return."

Now here is the way that Origin, Augustine, and Jerome interpreted the parable: The man himself stands for Adam. The word for man in Hebrew is *adam*, and ultimately he stands for all of mankind. The robbers stand for the devil and his angels who rob man of his original righteousness. The man is on his way from Jerusalem to Jericho. Jerusalem stands for the holy city, for Zion, and Jericho for the pagan world. The worship of the moon goddess took place in Jericho in pagan days. The man is clearly going in the path of fallenness. Along comes a priest. The priest is one who is bound by the law, stands for the law, and interprets the law. He, therefore, represents the law. So the law comes, but the law cannot bring man to his original righteousness. Then along comes the Levite. He stands for the Old Testament prophets. The prophets, too, cannot bring man to his original righteousness. Then along comes the good Samaritan. The good Samaritan is Jesus. The word Samaritan has the same basic root letters in Hebrew as the word guardian. And who is the guardian of our soul? Why, it is obviously Jesus. The good Samaritan puts oil and wine on the man's wounds. The oil stands for the anointing of the Spirit that takes place at one's baptism, and the wine represents the Lord's Supper. It is through these two sacraments given by Jesus that man learns God's grace. Then the man is placed on the Samaritan's donkey. What do all donkeys have? They have four legs. If they only had three legs, then they would not be able to walk very well. Of what do we have four? We have four Gospels. And so it is the four Gospels that will bring fallen man to safety. The man then arrives at the inn of safety. The inn of safety for believers is the church, and the innkeeper is Peter or the bishop of the church who has control of the sacraments. The two denarii that are given to take care of the man until the Samaritan returns are the Old and New Testament. It is then obvious that the return must be the second coming of Jesus.

The real difficulty with this interpretation is that it seems to miss the whole original context. The original context of this story is a man's question, "Who is my neighbor?" The story illustrates who a neighbor is and how a neighbor should behave.

In the fifth century AD Jerome continued to use the allegorical method of interpreting the parables. When asked, "Why do you use allegory?" he responded that he did it for two reasons. First "it is a challenge," and second "it grips the hearers."

One of the first to propose a break with this methodology was Martin Luther (1483–1546). He referred to allegorical interpretation as "a bunch of monkey tricks."

A crucial change in interpretative method came with Jülicher (1857–1938). His work on parables has been termed "the watershed in parable study." Jülicher tossed aside allegorical interpretation. He argued that a parable had one point of contact with the events surrounding it and that the parable made one point. That point was a moral, much like the fables. It was a time for a fresh look at the parables of Jesus.

The next scholar who made a significant contribution to the study of parables was C.H. Dodd (1884–1973). He argued that Jülicher had missed something essential. Folks of Jesus' day would never have crucified an itinerant preacher who went around preaching prudent, moral living. Dodd argued that parables had to be examined on two levels: the ministry of Jesus that originally produced the parable and the life of the early church that led to the parable being recorded. Dodd was never sure one could move back to the first level; one could only be sure of what was going on in the life of the early church. For Dodd all parables had an eschatological or end-time message.

Joachim Jeremias (1900–1979) was the next scholar to make a significant contribution. He argued that Dodd was wrong. The parables of Jesus were not primarily eschatological. He began by emphasizing Jewish backgrounds. The parables of Jesus were Jewish stories. Jeremias noted that Jesus' parables arose out of conflict and controversy. With parables, Jesus vindicated His gospel. Those parables, he contended, were Jesus' call to action.

Another recent interpreter, Frederick Houk Borsch in his book, *Many Things in Parables: Extravagant Stories of the New Community*, made an observation that is worth noting. He said that the parables of Jesus were ". . . designed to lure the hearers to become participants. They are invited to play parts. . . ."[1] We will see that his observation is both true and helpful.

---

[1] Frederick Houk Borsch, *Many Things in Parables: Extravagant Stories of the New Community* (Philadelphia: Fortress, 1988), p. 1.

FOUR KEY QUESTIONS

It has been suggested that explaining a parable is like explaining a joke. When one must explain it, the real punch of the parable or the joke is lost. While there is some truth in that observation, the reader today may need some guidance in reading a story spoken and then written so long ago to so different an audience.

I would suggest that we use four questions to drive our interpretation of the parables. These principles are gleaned from many scholars over the ages. They help the interpreter to stay true to the original meaning of the parable.

1. **What was happening in the life of Jesus that led to this parable?**

    Despite the claim of some, it is this author's belief that the parables of Jesus were not normally circulated without historical context. Jesus gave the parable to address a problem or answer a question, to vindicate His teaching about the kingdom.

2. **What was happening in the life of the early church in the author's day (Matthew's, Mark's, Luke's) that brought him to record this parable?**

    The problem of the evangelist's audience was not the Pharisees. His concern was not their attitude toward sinners and tax collectors, but his audience did face the problem of Judaizers and Gentile converts. The evangelists chose parables—and, for that matter, also miracles, discourses and events—which somehow spoke to their audiences. What were they hoping their audiences would learn and do?

3. **What's the point? What was the author trying to say to his audience? "When God reigns, . . ."**

    I cannot read a parable as if it were written to me today. I must seek the message of the author—the original author, Jesus, and the author of the Gospel, the evangelist. What were they trying to say?

4. **What is the message for me today? "If God is reigning in my life (my church), then . . ."**

    Only after answering the first three questions can I move to God's message to me today. Only then can we learn what it means for God to reign in our lives today. The reader should ask the question, "When God reigns in my life, in my church, how should I or we behave?"

LIVING IN GOD'S REIGN

1. Allegorize any parable of Jesus. Be as creative as you can be. Share your allegorical interpretations. Discuss how this method might miss the point.

2. Discuss how understanding the word "kingdom" as "reign or rule" can affect one's interpretation of biblical texts.

3. Look up the New Testament use of the word "kingdom" in a Bible concordance. Choose several passages where the word occurs and determine how the word is used in each passage. Try to find at least three instances of each usage.

4. Evaluate the quote from Frederick Borsch's book *Many Things in Parables.* The parables of Jesus were ". . . designed to lure the hearers to become participants. They are invited to play parts. . . ." Do you agree or disagree? Why?

5. Before really trying them out, what do you see as the strengths and weaknesses of the four questions the author of this book suggests for studying the parables?

CHAPTER 2

A Test Case

The goal of this chapter is to provide a test case for the principles set forth in the previous chapter for interpreting the parables of Jesus. We will try out these principles on a parable to demonstrate the questions and their viability.

The first question we will ask is "What was happening in the life of Jesus that led to this parable?" What had He just said? Who had just asked Him a question? Who had confronted Him with a problem? What was going on that caused Him to give the parable?

The second question is "What was happening in the life of the early church in the author's day (Matthew's, Mark's, or Luke's) that brought him to record the parable?" What would have caused the evangelist to preserve this parable for his audience?

The third question will be "What's the point?" What was the author (on both levels—Jesus to His audience and the evangelist to his) trying to say to his audience? When God reigns, what will happen?

The final question will then be "What's the message for me today?" If God is reigning in my life, my church, then what?

Parable of the Eleventh-Hour Workers

Our test case will be the parable of the Eleventh-Hour Workers in Matthew 20. It will be necessary to begin in Matthew 19 so that we can address the first question, "What was going on in the life of Jesus that caused Him to give the parable?"

This parable is especially appropriate for us to begin our study because Fee and Stuart in their book, *How to Read the Bible for All Its Worth*, have termed it a "Contextless" Parable.[2] While on occasion parables may have been

---

[2] Gordon D. Fee and Douglas Stuart, *How To Read the Bible for All Its Worth*, 2nd edition (Grand Rapids: Zondervan, 1993), p. 143.

grouped because of similar messages, it is this author's contention that they normally are transmitted with some sort of context. Without a context, the parables lose their meaning. McArthur and Johnston have demonstrated that the later rabbinic parables also circulated with some context that they call an illustrand, "the matter to be illustrated" by the parable.[3]

MATTHEW 19:16–20:16

[16]And someone came to Him and said, "Teacher, what good thing shall I do that I may obtain eternal life?" [17]And He said to him, "Why are you asking Me about what is good? There is *only* One who is good; but if you wish to enter into life, keep the commandments." [18]*Then* he *said to Him, "Which ones?" And Jesus said, "YOU SHALL NOT COMMIT MURDER; YOU SHALL NOT COMMIT ADULTERY; YOU SHALL NOT STEAL; YOU SHALL NOT BEAR FALSE WITNESS; [19]HONOR YOUR FATHER AND MOTHER; and YOU SHALL LOVE YOUR NEIGHBOR AS YOURSELF." [20]The young man said to Him, "All these things I have kept; what am I still lacking?" [21]Jesus said to him, "If you wish to be complete, go *and* sell your possessions and give to *the* poor, and you will have treasure in heaven; and come, follow Me." [22]But when the young man heard this statement, he went away grieving; for he was one who owned much property.

[23]And Jesus said to His disciples, "Truly I say to you, it is hard for a rich man to enter the kingdom of heaven. [24]"Again I say to you, it is easier for a camel to go through the eye of a needle, than for a rich man to enter the kingdom of God." [25]When the disciples heard *this*, they were very astonished and said, "Then who can be saved?" [26]And looking at *them* Jesus said to them, "With people this is impossible, but with God all things are possible."

[27]Then Peter said to Him, "Behold, we have left everything and followed You; what then will there be for us?" [28]And Jesus said to them, "Truly I say to you, that you who have followed Me, in the regeneration when the Son of Man will sit on His glorious throne, you also shall sit upon twelve thrones, judging the twelve tribes of Israel. [29]"And everyone who has left houses or brothers or sisters or father or mother or children or farms for My name's

---

[3] Harvey K. McArthur and Robert M. Johnston, *They Also Taught in Parables: Rabbinic Parables from the First Centuries of the Christian Era* (Grand Rapids: Zondervan, 1990), p. 109.

sake, will receive many times as much, and will inherit eternal life. [30]"But many *who are* first will be last; and *the* last, first.

[20:1]"For the kingdom of heaven is like a landowner who went out early in the morning to hire laborers for his vineyard. [2]"When he had agreed with the laborers for a denarius for the day, he sent them into his vineyard. [3]"And he went out about the third hour and saw others standing idle in the market place; [4]and to those he said, 'You also go into the vineyard, and whatever is right I will give you.' And *so* they went. [5]"Again he went out about the sixth and the ninth hour, and did the same thing. [6]"And about the eleventh *hour* he went out and found others standing *around*; and he said to them, 'Why have you been standing here idle all day long?' [7]"They said to him, 'Because no one hired us.' He said to them, 'You go into the vineyard too.' [8]"When evening came, the owner of the vineyard said to his foreman, 'Call the laborers and pay them their wages, beginning with the last *group* to the first.' [9]"When those *hired* about the eleventh hour came, each one received a denarius. [10]"When those *hired* first came, they thought that they would receive more; but each of them also received a denarius. [11]"When they received it, they grumbled at the landowner, [12]saying, 'These last men have worked *only* one hour, and you have made them equal to us who have borne the burden and the scorching heat of the day.' [13]"But he answered and said to one of them, 'Friend, I am doing you no wrong; did you not agree with me for a denarius? [14]"Take what is yours and go, but I wish to give to this last man the same as to you. [15]"Is it not lawful for me to do what I wish with what is my own? Or is your eye envious because I am generous?'

[16]"So the last shall be first, and the first last."

THE SITUATION

Through the centuries this parable has had many interesting allegorical interpretations. Irenaeus, toward the end of the second century, was convinced that the parable provided a picture of the various stages of salvation history. Each set of laborers (early morning, third hour, sixth hour, ninth hour, and eleventh hour) represented a different period beginning with creation down to the end time. This sort of interpretation does not, however, fit into the situation in Jesus' life that produced the parable.

The situation begins with someone coming to Jesus with a question, "Teacher, what good thing shall I do that I may obtain eternal life?" The man's question regarding eternal life was one very common in the first century AD. The rabbis debated which commandments were most significant and what one had to do to inherit eternal life. Jesus responds by giving the man some of the Ten Commandments. He cites from what is commonly called the second tablet of the Ten Commandments, those that deal with man's response to man. It is interesting that one of those commandments is omitted, "You shall not covet." We will learn that this commandment is the man's problem. To those commandments, Jesus adds, "You shall love your neighbor as yourself" (Lev. 19:18) to round out the man's obligation to those with whom he comes in contact.

The man responds by saying, "All these things I have kept, what am I still lacking?" Jesus' response leads us to believe that the young man is telling the truth. He tells the young man, "If you wish to be complete, go and sell your possessions and give to the poor and you will have treasure in heaven. Come and follow me." When the young man hears Jesus' words, he goes away grieving because he was one who owned much property.

If one puts together Matthew, Mark and Luke, the man in our story can be termed the Rich Young Ruler. He was apparently asking his question of Jesus sincerely. Jesus sees something special in this man. But the young man is unwilling to part with his possessions. His possessions matter so much to him that they become an obstacle for his entering the kingdom.

At this point Jesus tells His disciples that it is harder for a camel to go through the eye of a needle than for a rich man to enter the kingdom of God. It is interesting how students of the Bible have tried their best to understand this last figurative language of Jesus, this hyperbole, putting a camel through the eye of a needle. Some have suggested that Jesus may be referring to a gate in the city wall of Jerusalem. In fact, some of the older commentaries connect the saying of Jesus with this Eye of the Needle, a gate in the wall. To get the camel through the gate, one would have to get the camel down on its knees, take the load off, get it through the gate and then bring it up on the other side. The difficulty with such an interpretation is the fact that this gate in the wall dates from long after Jesus, from the middle ages. Others have suggested that there may be an error in transmission. They argue that Jesus originally used the Aramaic word for cable or rope, and a copyist somewhere along the line made a mistake so the text today reads camel. Getting a cable through a needle, though difficult would not be impossible if the needle has a big enough eye.

Jesus' disciples obviously see the difficulty with what He says. They fail to understand that Jesus is using a hyperbole. They respond, astonished, "Who then can be saved? You can't get a camel through the eye of a needle."

To the disciples' question Jesus responds, "With people this is impossible but with God all things are possible." Peter then says to him, "Behold we have left everything and followed you. What then will there be for us?" This question of Peter sets the stage for the parable that will follow in the next chapter. "We've left everything and followed you. If this man had left his possessions now, he would have been blessed. We've done that. We did it first. We have been at it longer than anybody else. What are we going to get out of this, Jesus?"

Jesus answers Peter's question by telling him, "Don't worry. You will be blessed. Whatever you give up for the kingdom you will gain much more. You may lose family, but you will gain a new family, You may lose property, but you will gain a treasure that is much greater and you will inherit eternal life."

THE INSIGHT

In verse 30, Jesus gives His hearers an insight into the parable He is about to tell them. "But many who are first will be last and the last first." This becomes very clear if one jumps to the next chapter and reads the verse that follows the parable, "So the last shall be first, and the first last" (Matt. 20:16). Since the parable is sandwiched between these verses, it becomes clear that Jesus is teaching something about the last becoming first and the first becoming last.

Jesus tells His disciples that the kingdom of heaven (God's reign) is like the story of a landowner and the workers who will harvest his grapes. The parable begins with this landowner, who is concerned about harvesting his grapes and needs workers to gather the grapes. He goes out to find workers early in the morning (we would assume before 6 A.M. since that is the time laborers would begin their work). He finds some men who are ready to work and strikes a deal that they will work that day for a denarius. A denarius was minimum wage for a day. It would have been the expected pay for such work.[4]

About the third hour or 9 A.M.,[5] the landowner, still in need of more workers, saw others standing idle in the market place, the place where one would expect to find such folks. He said to those he found there, "You also go into my vineyard to work, and whatever is right, I will give you." The assumption would be that they would be paid something less than a denarius. There were smaller coins in first-century Palestine, and so they went probably expecting to get about three-fourths of a denarius.

---

[4] Perhaps the best way for today's reader to get a feel for money in biblical times is to make the transition from minimum wage then to minimum wage today. At the release of this book, minimum wage is approximately $5.25 per hour. We work 8 hours per day. It is then best to think of a denarius as about $42. This method will work in any culture and any time to give one's audience a sense of the value of money in Jesus' day. This methodology will be used throughout the remainder of the book whenever amounts of money are mentioned.

[5] Jews counted time from the beginning of the work day, 6:00 A.M. Therefore, the third hour would be 9:00 A.M., the sixth hour 12 noon, the ninth hour 3:00 P.M., etc.

Again the landowner went out about the sixth hour (12:00 noon) and the ninth hour (3:00 P.M.) and did the same thing. Again he promises them, "Whatever's fair, I'll give you."

About the eleventh hour (5:00 P.M.), the landowner goes out yet one more time. This time he found still others standing around. He said to them, "Why have you been standing here idle all day long?" and they replied, "Because no one hired us." They were not lazy; they simply had not been given a chance to work. He said to them, "You go into the vineyard, too." Normally laborers worked from six until six. There is only one hour left to work. It is the cooler part of the day. The breeze has come up; the sun isn't shining quite so brightly. He tells these folks, "I want you to work as well." They assume that they will receive some money for their work, but they would have assumed that they would not receive a denarius. "Whatever's fair, I'm going to give you." These men get an opportunity to work, and they go off to work.

When evening came, the owner of the vineyard said to his foreman, "Call the laborers and pay them their wages beginning with the last group to the first." It is important that they are paid from the last group to the first. Why? The parable is about last first, first last (Matt. 19:30; 20:16). But also it would ruin the story if those who had worked all day were paid first. If the laborers who had worked the longest were paid first, they would have gone home, never knowing what the others received. It is significant that Jesus does not mention those who came to work at the third, sixth and ninth hour. This provides a subtle warning to those who would allegorize the parable and make each set of workers stand for something.

When those hired about the eleventh hour came, the compensation they received was a denarius. In the previous chapter we noted the contention of Borsch that the parables of Jesus were ". . . designed to lure the hearers to become participants. They are invited to play parts. . . ."[6] The hearer/reader is tempted to play the part of those who had worked hard all day. When those hired first came, they thought they would receive more. But each of them also received a denarius. Now you can kind of imagine how this would have worked. If you had been working all day long and folks who had worked one hour received $42, you might well have done the mathematics $42 times 12. You might have assumed you would receive $504.

Those who had worked all day also received a denarius. They began to grumble at the landowner's saying, "These men have worked only one hour, and you have made them equal to us and who have born the burden of the day

---

[6] Frederick Houk Borsch, *Many Things in Parables: Extravagant Stories of the New Community* (Philadelphia: Fortress, 1988), p. 1.

and the scorching heat of the day." Their comment is basically, "It's not fair."

The master answered their complaint. "Friend I am doing you no wrong. Did you not agree with me for a denarius? Take what is yours and go. But I wish to give to this man the same as to you. Is it not lawful for me to do what I wish with what is my own or is your eye envious because I am generous?" Notice that the parable ends in the same way it began. "But many who are first will be last; and the last, first." And now the admonition, "So the last shall be first, and the first last."

THE APPLICATION

We begin our study of a parable by asking first, "What was happening in the life of Jesus that led to this parable?' This time it is Peter's question that produced the parable, "We have left everything to follow you; what will there be for us?" Jesus gives the parable to answer Peter's question.

Our second question we ask is "What was happening in the life of the early church in the author's day, Matthew's, Mark's or Luke's, that brought him to record this parable?" In this text that answer to that question is not terribly difficult. In Matthew's day, the big problem with comparison was the Jews comparing themselves with Gentiles. It did not seem fair for those new upstarts to become acceptable believers without circumcision and law keeping. After all, Jewish Christians had been doing that all their lives. Perhaps Gentile Christians should at least be relegated to secondary status. It just wasn't fair! As Matthew addresses his Jewish audience, He wants to help them understand the nature of the kingdom.

What is the point? What was the author trying to say to his audience? When God reigns, what? It would seem that Jesus was saying to Peter, "Don't compare yourself with others, just serve." That language, "first last, last first," is language of service and humility throughout the New Testament. Matthew, in turn, was saying to his audience that Jews should not be comparing themselves with those new converts from among the Gentiles. They should simply serve.

What is the message for the reader today? If God's reigning in my life or my church, then what? Typically, folks have interpreted this parable as though it were addressing deathbed confessions. While it may well address that issue, it would seem that it has a much broader application that we may be missing. We must carry out the tasks given to us and not be concerned with others and their rewards. We must move beyond, "It's not fair."

This was a very difficult lesson for Peter to learn. In John chapter 21 after Jesus has asked Peter three times, "Do you love me?" Jesus and Peter are walking along the beach together. He tells Peter that he has always gotten up in the morning and put his own belt on and gone where he wanted to go, but the day would come when others would bind him and they would lead him where they didn't want to go. John goes on to say that this signified the kind of death that Peter would face. Peter's response was, "Lord if that's good for me, I think the beloved disciple, John, ought to get a little of that as well." Jesus' response to Peter is "If I want him to remain until I come again, what is that to you?" Peter is still comparing himself with another person. It is a lesson that is hard to learn. Later there will come on the scene a new apostle, Paul, who was not a part of the original group. How will Peter and the others respond to him? In Acts 10, Peter was not anxious to go to the house of Cornelius, to those Gentiles. He had not seen that God had a place for everyone. The lesson is a tough one for us to learn.

LIVING IN GOD'S REIGN

1. Now that we have tested them, what do you see as the strengths and weaknesses of the four questions the author of this book suggests for studying the parables?
2. How did you previously understand the parable of the eleventh-hour workers?
3. Has your understanding of this parable changed?
4. Discuss the meaning of this parable for the contemporary church.

CHAPTER 3

Why Parables?
To Confuse or to Make Clear?

Jesus teaches primarily with parables in the Synoptic Gospels (Matthew, Mark, and Luke). Just why does Jesus choose this method? After Jesus tells the crowds who are following Him the parable of the sower, His disciples ask that very question (Matt. 13:10-17; Mark 4:10-12; Luke 8:9-10). Jesus explains the parable and uses it to indicate why He teaches with parables. For that reason the parable of the sower is sometimes called "a parable of parables." It becomes the paradigm for understanding parables and Jesus' use of them. Although this might well be a good place to begin a study in the parables of Jesus, this author shies away from such a start because, in this parable, the allegorical element is so significant. The danger in beginning here is that the reader may be tempted to look too intently for allegorical elements, may want to have every element of a parable stand for something, and may begin to view all parables as allegories. There is a significant difference between suggesting that parables are allegories and acknowledging that parables are allegorical or have allegorical elements. It is, however, imperative that we examine this parable to learn why Jesus used parables. Discovering His intent will affect the way we read the parables.

Parable of the Sower

The parable of the sower is found in Mark 4:1-34, Luke 8:4-18, and with Matthew's account beginning in 13:1–23:

> "That day Jesus went again out of the house and was sitting by the sea. And large crowds gathered to Him, so He got into a boat and sat down, and the whole crowd was standing on the beach. And He spoke many things to them in parables, saying, 'Behold the sower went out to sow. . . .'"

Today we are concerned about yield. How much can I expect to make from my investment in the stock market? What interest will I receive on my money market account? Jesus' parable addresses yield as well. What yield should the apostles expect when the kingdom is proclaimed?

The crowds pressed Jesus as He stood by the Sea of Galilee. He was forced into a small fishing boat and that boat became His pulpit. The traditional site of this parable is a spot on the Sea of Galilee from which one could see fields of wheat. Some have imagined that a man might well have been in his field sowing seed so that Jesus had before Him a wonderful visual aid. A man would walk through his field broadcasting seed to the right and left.

". . . and as he sowed, some seeds fell beside the road, and the birds came and ate them up."

Now the seed that fell beside the road is on the walkway perhaps between fields, the path where people have walked over and over again. The ground is beaten down. The seed falls there and lands on top of that hard-packed soil. It simply rests there, and the birds come and eat it. The situation is a little like what many of us experience when we try to plant grass in our front yards. We may discover that we do more to feed birds than to grow grass.

"Others fell on the rocky places, where they did not have much soil; and immediately they sprang up, because they had no depth of soil. But when the sun had risen, they were scorched; and because they had no root, they withered away."

This soil is rocky not because it has many rocks in it but because it has a rock bed beneath it. There is a very shallow layer of soil and beneath that a rock ledge. It does not have much depth of soil. Because there is a rock ledge beneath, the soil is heated by the sun. The warmth of the sun heats the rock, and, in turn, the rock keeps the soil warm. Perhaps this soil would be warmer than soil that had more depth. This soil is also very moist. During the rainy season, the moisture would stay on top of rock. This soil has everything necessary to provide the seed with a quick start. The seed that falls here sprouts immediately, but, when the sun has risen, the new growth is scorched. The new plant cannot sink down roots; it withers away. Such a growing environment is typical of many places in east Tennessee or in Palestine.

"Others fell among the thorns, and the thorns came up and choked them out."

Anyone with gardening experience can appreciate what Jesus is here describing. Thorns and thistles seem to thrive in places where crops that we wish to grow struggle. They can squeeze out the good plants.

> **"And others fell on the good soil and yielded a crop, some a hundredfold, some sixty, and some thirty. He who has ears, let him hear."**

A very good crop in Jesus' day would have been twenty fold, twenty bushels of wheat for every bushel of seed sown. Thirty, and sixty, and hundred fold would have been amazing, unbelievable growth. Notice that last phrase, "He who has ears to hear let him hear." Jesus offers a call for those with hearts that desire to understand to understand.

I have always been tempted to change the name of this parable and call it "the parable of soils" because the focus seems to be on the four different types of soil, each of which represents a different hearer. It was not until I discovered that it was Jesus who gave the parable its name (Matt. 13:18, "Hear then the parable of the sower") that I decided I should reconsider that proposal. Even the name He gives the parable may be informative. Jesus may be telling the disciples what kind of response they should expect when they sow the seeds of the kingdom. One can wrongly assume that, if the gospel is proclaimed well enough, everyone will respond in faith. One can also be easily discouraged when responses are not as favorable as one might hope.

THE RATIONALES

> **"And the disciples came and said to Him, 'Why do You speak to them in parables?' Jesus answered them, 'To you it has been granted to know the mysteries of the kingdom of heaven, but to them it has not been granted. For whoever has, to him *more* shall be given and he will have an abundance; but whoever does not have, even what he has shall be taken away from him.'"**

Matthew reports two rationales for the parables, one related to their function for outsiders and one related to their function for the disciples. Outsiders will see wonderful stories but will never get the message. That may well be what has just occurred. The crowds hear Jesus' story about the sower and say, "Yes, that is exactly what happens when one sows seed in a field. The seed falls in various places. One must certainly be careful to make sure it falls on good ground." The disciples, on the other hand, because they have the right kind of heart, will have wonderful mysteries revealed to them.

Walvoord says that Jesus deliberately chose the parabolic method of teaching at this time in His ministry in order to withhold further truth about Himself and the kingdom from the crowds. They were deaf to His claims and irresponsive to His demands so He simply bypasses them. When addressing the unbelieving multitude, Jesus speaks only in parables, which He interprets to His disciples in private.[7]

Walvoord might mislead the reader into thinking a special time has arisen now in Matthew 13 for this to occur. It is doubtful that Matthew 13 contains the first of Jesus' parables. Matthew has already recorded parables in chapters 7, 9, and 11. As Carson has suggested, rising opposition may have encouraged Jesus to a greater use of parables.[8] Parables, though, are not restricted to Jesus' ministry to outsiders. He used them positively for the believers, as well as for the disciples.

MATTHEW 13:13

"Therefore I speak to them in parables; because while seeing they do not see, and while hearing they do not hear, nor do they understand."

Matthew's treatment here is much longer than Mark's or Luke's. He spends considerably more time explaining His use of parables (Matt. 13:11-17 versus Mark 4:11-12 and Luke 8:10). Here, Matthew includes Jesus' quotation of an Old Testament Scripture, and in Matthew the text is structured with greater care than either Mark or in Luke. Jesus' answer, on the surface, seems to be very harsh. At least one of the functions of parables is to conceal the truth or at least to present it in a veiled way, so that not everyone will catch on. The disciples are learning about the "mysteries" of the kingdom (NIV "secrets" of the kingdom). Jesus' meaning of that phrase is not explained. A mystery is something once hidden and now revealed. Jesus tells the disciples, "This mystery has been revealed to you, My disciples, but not to them, the crowds." What is revealed is that God's reign is now breaking into the world. There is still much the disciples do not know or understand, but they have insight that the rest of the world lacks.

Mark's Gospel is even more enigmatic than Matthew's or Luke's at this point.

---

[7] John F. Walvoord, *Matthew: Thy Kingdom Come* (Chicago: Moody, 1974).
[8] Donald A. Carson, *Matthew*, Expositor's Bible Commentary (Grand Rapids: Zondervan).

MARK 4:10-12

As soon as He was alone, His followers, along with the twelve, *began* asking Him *about* the parables. And He was saying to them, "To you has been given the mystery of the kingdom of God, but those who are outside get everything in parables, so that WHILE SEEING, THEY MAY SEE AND NOT PERCEIVE, AND WHILE HEARING, THEY MAY HEAR AND NOT UNDERSTAND, OTHERWISE THEY MIGHT RETURN AND BE FORGIVEN."

Later in the chapter Mark explains:

MARK 4:33-34

With many such parables He was speaking the word to them, so far as they were able to hear it; and He did not speak to them without a parable; but He was explaining everything privately to His own disciples.

A significant issue in our text is Jesus' statement that He uses parables "so that" His audience will not "perceive," "understand," "return," and "be forgiven."[9] Jesus' use of "so that" or "in order that they might not" might be seen as implying that the parables blind outsiders and that this is to be taken as a function of divine election. Jesus purposefully rules out some hearers. Matthew, however, uses a different Greek word[10] translated "because." Jesus speaks here in parables "because" the people are spiritually insensitive. The word Mark has chosen can express either purpose (Jesus speaks in parables with the purpose of concealing) or result (Jesus speaks in parables and the result is a concealed message). It would seem when comparing Matthew and Luke that Mark may not be expressing purpose but rather result. Jesus uses parables and the "result" is that people do not see. They don't hear and they don't understand.

Though the crowd sees, they do not really see. Though they hear, they do not really hear. The parable of the sower teaches that the kingdom advances slowly, with varied responses to its proclamation. The parable says something about parables. People will have varied responses to both the proclamation of the kingdom and the parables used in that proclamation. This parable challenges hearers to ask themselves, "What kind of soil am I?" or "What kind of hearer am I?" The parable of the sower serves as Jesus' answer to the question, "Why do you use parables?" Jesus answers the question by saying, "The para-

---

[9] The Greek word rendered "so that" is here *hina* (ἵνα) followed by Greek verbs in the subjunctive.

[10] Matthew uses *hoti* (ὅτι).

ble I just told you tells why I use parables. I have different hearers; some will understand; they will soak it all up. They will bear fruit. For others it will bounce off. For some it will last only for a while. Those folks with hardened hearts will not understand it; they will lose what they have. Those who have ears to hear will perceive and experience the dawning of the Messianic Age." Jesus did not use parables to hide His message from all. Those with tender hearts would understand. In Matthew 13:34-35, He makes it clear that parables were designed to make things hidden clear (see pages 131-132).

In Matthew, Jesus continues His explanation with a quotation from Isaiah. He informs His disciples that this passage is being fulfilled. One needs to be careful not to misunderstand Jesus' statement at this point. The passage was fulfilled—that is, it occurred—in Isaiah's day. Isaiah did not have in mind Jesus' use of parables when he first gave that word from the Lord. The Lord was telling Isaiah what he could expect in terms of response to his preaching from the people in his day. That passage is now being "fulfilled"—that is, filled full of meaning—in Jesus' day. It now really makes sense. Isaiah informs his hearers:

MATTHEW 13:14B-15 *(Isaiah 6:9-10)*

"YOU WILL KEEP ON HEARING, BUT WILL NOT UNDERSTAND; YOU WILL KEEP ON SEEING, BUT WILL NOT PERCEIVE; FOR THE HEART OF THIS PEOPLE HAS BECOME DULL, WITH THEIR EARS THEY SCARCELY HEAR, AND THEY'VE CLOSED THEIR EYES, OTHERWISE THEY WOULD SEE WITH THEIR EYES, HEAR WITH THEIR EARS, AND UNDERSTAND WITH THEIR HEART AND RETURN, AND I WOULD HEAL THEM."

Isaiah has been given a charge to preach but God tells him not to expect a favorable response. It is not really a desirable task because inevitably the people to whom he will preach are callused. It is the same in Jesus' day. The context of Isaiah 6:9-10 reveals that the dullness of the Jews will continue "until the cities lie ruined and the fields ruined and ravaged and the land is utterly forsaken and though a tenth remains in the land it will be laid waste." Jesus continues in Matthew 13:16-17:

"But blessed are your eyes, because they see; and your ears, because they hear. For truly I say to you that many prophets and righteous men desired to see what you see, and did not see *it*, and to hear what you hear, and did not hear *it*."

The disciples were blessed by God and were privileged above the crowd, but also above many prophets and righteous people of ages gone by. The prophets and saints of days gone by longed to see and hear what the disciples were seeing and hearing, but they did not. The reference is obviously to Old Testament prophets and to people we read about in the Gospels like Simeon and Anna, those who could appreciate the coming of the kingdom.

THE EXPLANATION

With the exhortation, "Hear the parable of the sower," Jesus begins to explain the parable. Jesus' interpretation does seem very allegorical because certain things do stand for certain things. The difference between this parable's allegoric elements and its being a true allegory rests in the way one learns what represents what. From the context one learns what they stand for what. One is not left to his own imagination to develop these relationships.

MATTHEW 13:19

"When anyone hears the word of the kingdom and does not understand it, the evil *one* comes and snatches away what has been sown in his heart. This is the one on whom the seed was sown beside the road."

Notice the seed is the word and the one who snatches it, the birds in the parable, is the devil. This soil represents the one who is, as Vallet describes him, "hard on the outside."[11] Jesus was referring to those who would hear His teaching and see His miracles but, because of their set ideas and beliefs, would never come to faith. They are the hard-headed hearers, those who hear the message but have it simply bounce off. They are people whose lifestyles, systems of priorities, and predetermined sets of values get in the way of responding to the good news of the kingdom.

MATTHEW 13:20-21

"The one on whom seed was sown on the rocky places, this is the man who hears the word and immediately receives it with joy; yet he has no *firm* root in himself, but is *only* temporary, and when affliction or persecution arises because of the word, immediately he falls away."

Most have seen those who make a grand start as Christians but do not last when the persecution gets tough. There are problems in their marriage so they

---

[11] Ronald E. Vallet, *Stepping Stones of the Steward*, 2nd ed. (Grand Rapids: Eerdmans, 1994), p. 33.

abandon the marriage and their faith. They struggle to make a living and give up their call. They have a terrible event in their life and feel God is to blame for allowing it and leave behind their Christian walk. All have responded to a call from God but leave behind that call and their commitment.

MATTHEW 13:22

"And the one on whom seed was sown among the thorns, this is the man who hears the word, and the worry of the world and the deceitfulness of wealth choke the word, and it becomes unfruitful."

Weedy ground is a curse for any gardener. The weeds and thorns take all the nutrients that the plants need to grow. Here is someone who has conflicting priorities. This person is too concerned about the things of this world, money, possessions, position. Such a person becomes unfruitful. All his energy is spent making money, trying to improve rank, and seeking to accumulate possessions. There is nothing left to spend on developing kingdom life.

MATTHEW 13:23

"And the one on whom seed was sown on the good soil, this is the man who hears the word and understands it; who indeed bears fruit and brings forth, some a hundredfold, some sixty, and some thirty."

The good soil produces varying amounts of fruit depending on peoples' abilities. But notice that all the amounts indicate magnificent responses. Everyone who responds positively to the message of the kingdom will develop in amazing ways that exceed human expectations. Again, the text indicates that people will respond to the message of Jesus differently.

This parable seems to provide two different messages to two different audiences. To those outside the twelve there is a call to examine what kind of hearer one is. As noted earlier the temptation here is to call this parable the parable of the soils because those soils represent four different kinds of hearers. It is interesting that Jesus is the one who called the parable the parable of the sower. To the disciples, Jesus may well be telling this parable so that they will understand why they do not get the same result from everyone. When you go out to sow, you expect folks to respond to the message differently. It was so with Isaiah, it was so with Jesus, and so it will be with you.

LIVING IN GOD'S REIGN

1. It seems that Jesus may have had two audiences in mind when He gave the parable of the sower. What was the message Jesus intended for the twelve when He gave the parable?

2. If He had a different message in mind for the crowd who listened to the parable of the sower, what do you think Jesus wanted them to learn or reflect on in the parable?

3. Discuss the following statement: The parables of Jesus are intended both to reveal and to hide.

4. Discuss Isaiah 6:9-10 in its original context. What did it mean to Isaiah and his audience? How does it apply to Jesus and His use of parables?

CHAPTER 4

When God Reigns, I'll Know and Appreciate His Grace

Although the word grace never appears in the parables of Jesus, many of them teach its significance. In many of His parables, Jesus illuminates God's grace and calls disciples to appreciate that grace. This chapter will focus on some of those parables.

Parable of the Unforving Servant

The parable of the unforgiving servant occurs in Matthew 18:21-35. To set the stage for the parable one must, however, begin at verse 15. The narrative context for the parable begins:

MATTHEW 18:15-20

[15]"If your brother sins, go and show him his fault in private; if he listens to you, you have won your brother. [16]"But if he does not listen *to you*, take one or two more with you, so that BY THE MOUTH OF TWO OR THREE WITNESSES EVERY FACT MAY BE CONFIRMED. [17]"If he refuses to listen to them, tell it to the church; and if he refuses to listen even to the church, let him be to you as a Gentile and a tax collector. [18]"Truly I say to you, whatever you bind on earth shall have been bound in heaven; and whatever you loose on earth shall have been loosed in heaven.

[19]"Again I say to you, that if two of you agree on earth about anything that they may ask, it shall be done for them by My Father who is in heaven. [20]"For where two or three have gathered together in My name, I am there in their midst."

From the context, Jesus is dealing primarily with the twelve disciples. He informs them that, if one brother sins against another, then the brother who has been sinned against is to try to resolve the problem with his brother alone. If that effort fails, he should takes along some witnesses. If that too fails, he should bring it before the whole group. Although the word *ecclēsia* is generally translated "church," in context it might be best to translate it "assembly" or "group." Jesus is clearly addressing a problem among His small group of believers. Matthew's use of the word may give insights into his hermeneutic or application of the text. Jesus' instructions to His disciples provide the plan that Matthew expects believers to follow in the church. If the sinner does not listen to the group, then he should be treated as a Gentile and a tax collector. In an attempt to get rid of gender specific language the New Revised Standard Version goes a little too far in this text by rendering "If your brother sins . . ." as "If a fellow church member sins. . . ." The attempt to get rid of sexist language misses the fact that Jesus is talking to His disciples and not to the church, producing an anachronism.

Jesus continues His instruction by telling the disciples, "Whatever you bind on earth shall have been bound in heaven, whatever you loose on earth shall have been loosed in heaven." At this point the New American Standard Bible Update renders the Greek original in a very literal sense. Most translations render the Greek, "Whatever you bind . . . will be bound. . . . Whatever you loose . . . will be loosed." Such a translation would lead one to believe that Jesus is telling His disciples, "Whatever you say, goes." Instead Jesus is telling them, "You will be making the right decision. Your decision will be the one already deemed right in heaven." He is informing them in the context that they will make the right decision in regard to brothers who err. His instructions continue, "Again I say to you, that if two of you agree on earth about anything that they may ask, it shall be done for them by My Father who is in heaven."

Again, the context concerns the question, "What do we do about this brother?" Jesus' concern is not the public assembly. He is not discussing how many folks must be present to take the Lord's Supper on any given Sunday. He rather is telling the twelve, "I want you to realize that, when you make these decisions as a community, I will be with you."

It is at this point, though, that Peter asks an important question that leads Jesus to teach His disciples with the parable that follows. The words of Jesus had caught Peter's attention. He was reasoning through what Jesus had said, "All right. My brother sins against me, I go to him. He will probably repent. If that doesn't work, I take two or three witnesses. If he didn't repent the first time, he'll surely repent this time. If I get the whole church involved, he will certainly repent then. I'll be expected to forgive him. Man, this is going to get old really quick." So Peter asks Jesus the question with which he has been struggling.

> [21]**Then Peter came and said to Him, "Lord, how often shall my brother sin against me and I forgive him? Up to seven times?"** [22]**Jesus said to him, "I do not say to you, up to seven times, but up to seventy times seven.**

Peter undoubtedly thought Jesus would commend him for his generosity. Rabbis of his day suggested one should forgive twice before demanding vengeance. Jesus' response shows that He demanded a higher standard. "I do not say to you up to seven times but up to seventy times seven." The Greek original is a bit ambiguous and could say seventy-seven times or seventy times seven. No matter which number Jesus suggested, He is demanding forgiveness to a degree far beyond what Peter could have imagined, 490 times or 77 times.

It is at this juncture that Jesus shares a parable with His disciples. That parable seeks to answer Peter's question in a very graphic manner.

> [23]**"For this reason the kingdom of heaven may be compared to a king who wished to settle accounts with his slaves.** [24]**"When he had begun to settle *them*, one who owed him ten thousand talents was brought to him.** [25]**"But since he did not have *the means* to repay, his lord commanded him to be sold, along with his wife and children and all that he had, and repayment be made.** [26]**"So the slave fell *to the ground* and prostrated himself before him, saying, 'Have patience with me and I will repay you everything.'** [27]**"And the lord of that slave felt compassion and released him and forgave him the debt."**

The king had allowed his slaves to borrow and invest his money. The time came for him to settle his accounts with them. One slave who owed him 10,000 talents was brought to him. Since the slave had no way to repay the debt, the king commanded him to be sold, along with his wife, children and property and that repayment be made. The man's debt was an unusually large one. At this point, we learn something about the parables of Jesus. Parables differ from fables in that they could happen. Notice the operative word is "could" and not "would." It is very unlikely that a master would ever loan his slave 10,000 talents. If a talent is to be seen as 6,000 denarii, then the amount owed in terms of spending money in the United States today would be figured by multiplying 10,000 talents times 6,000 denarii times $42 (minimum wage for one day's work in the United States in 2004). The value would be approximately $2,520,000,000—$2.5 billion. Although such a debt was possible, it was unlikely that any master would loan a slave $2,520,000,000. After all, a slave does not even earn minimum wage. In this parable the amount the slave owes is exorbitantly high to drive home Jesus' point. Some have even suggested emending the parable, so that the man would have owed only 10,000 denarii to make the debt more reasonable, but the point of Jesus was that this debt was unimaginably large. Since the slave obviously lacks the means to repay, his lord commanded him to be sold along with his wife and children and all that he had and repayment be made. Even that would produces "pennies on the dollar" in terms of repayment.

So the slave fell to the ground and prostrated himself before the king saying, "Have patience with me, I will repay everything." Obviously he could never have repaid the debt. If he were being paid as a slave minimum wage (remember slaves were not paid wages), it would have taken more than 200,000 years working 300 days per year and spending none of his income on his own needs to repay that kind of debt. We learn that the lord felt compassion on his slave and forgave all $2,460,000,000 of the debt.

What a marvelous story of forgiveness. But the story does not end there.

> [28]**"But that slave went out and found one of his fellow slaves who owed him a hundred denarii; and he seized him and** *began* **to choke** *him,* **saying, 'Pay back what you owe.'** [29]**"So his fellow slave fell** *to the ground* **and** *began* **to plead with him, saying, 'Have patience with me and I will repay you.'** [30]**"But he was unwilling and went and threw him in prison until he should pay back what was owed.** [31]**"So when his fellow slaves saw what had happened, they were deeply grieved and came and reported to their lord all that had happened.** [32]**"Then summoning him, his lord said to him, 'You wicked slave, I forgave you all the debt because you pleaded with me.** [33]**"Should you not also have had mercy on your fellow slave, in the same way that I had mercy on you?'** [34]**"And his lord, moved with anger, handed him over to the torturers until he should repay all that was owed him.** [35]**"My heavenly Father will also do the same to you, if each of you does not forgive his brother from your heart."**

The slave decided it was time for him to collect on a debt. He went out and found one of his fellow slaves who owed him one hundred denarii. He seized him, began choking him, and said, "Pay back what you owe!" One must not misunderstand the size of that debt by thinking it either too large or too small.

Following the same mathematical formula, 100 denarii times $42 would produce a debt of $4,200. That is still a sizable debt. Most of us, if we were owed $4,200, would be anxious to collect that debt. So the first slave says, "Pay me back what you owe!" His debtor's response is much the same as his had been to the king, "Have patience with me, I will repay." This slave was unwilling either to give his fellow slave time to repay or to forgive him his debt. He went back and threw his fellow slave into prison until he should pay back what was owed him.

When the other slaves in the household saw what had happened, they quickly saw the inconsistency. They were deeply grieved so they reported everything to their lord. The king called in the slave he had earlier forgiven and said to him, "You wicked slave, I forgave you all that debt because you pleaded with me. Should you not also have had mercy on your fellow slave in the same way that I had mercy on you?" Responding in a very reasonable way, the king was moved with anger and handed the slave over to the torturers until his entire debt be repaid. It is again obvious that the debt would never be repaid. Despite the claims of some, this text was not designed to teach about purgatory and how long one must stay there. The master will never be repaid. The slave would be in torment forever.

Jesus clarifies the message of the parable with a single sentence, "My heavenly Father will also do the same to you if each of you does not forgive his brother *from your heart*". Notice the phrase "from your heart." It is the key idea in this text. That phrase answers the question that Peter asked of Jesus. Peter had asked, "How many times must I forgive my brother?" *From your heart* indicates that the issue is not how many times one must forgive. It is forgiving *from the heart*. When one does that, he stops counting.

When our brothers and sisters sin against us, it really hurts. The debt is significant. But that hurt, that debt, pales when compared to the hurt we have given the Father, the debt we owe Him. When God reigns in our lives, we will appreciate God's grace and then demonstrate that grace to others."

Parable of the Two Debtors

My interest in this parable goes back several years. When I began teaching at Lipscomb University, perhaps in my second year as a professor, I had a young man in a freshman Bible class who was my age. Everyone else in the class was eighteen, all freshmen studying Luke's Gospel. This young man was fifteen years older than the other students in the class. He had gone through all sorts of difficulty. He had been a drunkard, a drug addict, a drug dealer. He had told me that one time he had in his right hand one million dollars in cash and in his left one million dollars in drugs. On one occasion he had been stabbed seven times in his chest. As we studied Luke's Gospel, he was always asking wonderful questions, questions about the grace of God and what the grace of God really meant. Another young man in the class came up after class one day with an interesting comment. He said, "I wish I had the appreciation for God's grace that he (the older student) has." The next day I had the older student to tell his story. He told of his rebellious life, of drugs and alcohol and sex. He explained that he had been brought up by a Christian family but had never been a Christian. He had been kicked out of three Christian colleges and that many state schools. He was ready to end it all. He had been married; his first wife had divorced him. She was an alcoholic. One day driving drunk, she had killed herself, leaving him with a daughter to raise. He married a second time, and by that woman he had two sons. She was a beautiful stewardess and slept around all the time. Life was miserable. She had then divorced him to have her freedom. One day, he decided that he had had all he could take. He would simply end it all. He headed to a hotel in downtown Nashville with a gun intending to kill himself. He placed one bullet in a chamber of the gun, put the gun next to his head, spun the cylinder and pulled the trigger every hour on the hour, for seven hours. Amazingly he did not kill himself. The hammer never ended up behind the chamber with the bullet. Despite the alcohol and drugs, he was convinced God had something in mind for him. He decided to call a local preacher. The preacher studied with him, and he was baptized. After becoming a Christian, he met a wonderful Christian young lady. She had encouraged him to come to Lipscomb to study Bible and to complete a bachelor's degree in Bible. Ultimately he would complete a Master's degree in Bible. He understood the grace of God in a wonderful way. He understood it so well because he recognized the size of his debt before God.

After he had shared his story with my class, one of the students came up to me and asked the question, "Is it better to be bad and then be good than to always be pretty good? You know I've been raised a Christian, and I've never been bad. I've never tried drugs, and I've never drunk. Since I was never really bad, I'm not sure I appreciate the grace of God like this other fellow does. Is it better to be bad and then be good than to always be pretty good?" His question was very interesting. Perhaps by the providence of God, the text that we were to study the next day in the class was the parable of the two debtors.

LUKE 7:36

"Now one of the Pharisees was requesting Him to dine with him, and He entered the Pharisee's house and reclined *at the table*."

Notice the Pharisee invited Jesus to dine with him even though he neither agreed theologically with Jesus nor appreciated His association with social outcasts. After all, Jesus was a celebrity. Folks always want to rub elbows with a celebrity. Whether or not one is a Republican, if a Republican President came in town, he probably would be glad to eat with him.

> [37]**"And there was a woman in the city who was a sinner; and when she learned that He was reclining** *at the table* **in the Pharisee's house, she brought an alabaster vial of perfume,** [38]**and standing behind** *Him* **at His feet, weeping, she began to wet His feet with her tears, and kept wiping them with the hair of her head, and kissing His feet and anointing them with the perfume."**

The reader is not informed what kind of sinner this woman was. Many have assumed she was a prostitute. There is nothing that necessarily indicates that. Some have seen the fact that she will later let her hair down as an indication of this. She was a sinner. For a Pharisee, like Simon, anyone who was a non-Pharisee would be deemed a sinner. Such a person did not live by Pharisee standards and was, therefore, not ritually and morally pure.

Jesus was reclining at table. That was the norm. One would lean against a pillow on his left arm and eat with his right arm. Jesus' feet were not under the table as one would expect today. The woman did not have to crawl under the table because Jesus' feet were sticking out behind Him. She went behind Him and wet His feet with her tears, wiped them with her hair, kissed His dirty feet and anointed them with perfume.

> [39]**"Now when the Pharisee who had invited Him saw this, he said to himself, 'If this man were a prophet, He would know who and what sort of person this woman is who is touching Him, that she is a sinner.'** [40]**And Jesus answered him, . . ."**

Simon begins reasoning to himself. It is interesting that Simon has not said anything but Jesus answers him. It is as if Jesus hears him thinking.

> [40]**"And Jesus answered him, 'Simon, I have something to say to you.' And he replied, 'Say it, Teacher.'"**

It is at this point that Jesus gives Simon a parable to make His point clear.

> [41]**"A moneylender had two debtors: one owed five hundred denarii, and the other fifty.** [42]**"When they were unable to repay, he graciously forgave them both. So which of them will love him**

more?' ⁴³Simon answered and said, 'I suppose the one whom he forgave more.' And He said to him, 'You have judged correctly.'"

Notice the size of the debts: $42 times 500 denarii = $21,000; $42 times 50 denarii = $2,100. Each of the men owed sizable sums. One had ten times the debt of the other. It is important to see that both men had debts they could not repay.

Jesus' question was not which one *should* love the moneylender more but which one *will* love him more. Knowing human kind as we know human kind, which one *will* love him more?

> ⁴⁴"Turning toward the woman, He said to Simon, 'Do you see this woman? I entered your house; you gave Me no water for My feet, but she has wet My feet with her tears and wiped them with her hair. ⁴⁵You gave Me no kiss; but she, since the time I came in, has not ceased to kiss My feet. ⁴⁶You did not anoint My head with oil, but she anointed My feet with perfume.'"

Normally, in biblical times, when someone would come to your house, you would greet him with a kiss, usually a kiss on each cheek. You would arrange to have his feet washed and his head anointed with oil. But Simon gave Jesus no kiss, did not wash His feet, and did not anoint His head with oil. He had done none of the normal things that one does to show hospitality. He had shown no real appreciation for his guest. It was as though he had done Jesus a favor by inviting Him to his house. He felt no special honor in entertaining the Son of God. He had missed what was really important.

> ⁴⁷"For this reason I say to you, her sins, which are many, have been forgiven, for she loved much; but he who is forgiven little, loves little."

Jesus did not say her sins "*are* forgiven," but "*have been* forgiven." He uses the past perfect tense; it happened in the past and has an abiding consequence on the present. Her actions show that she recognizes a great debt and a marvelous forgiveness.

> ⁴⁸Then He said to her, "Your sins have been forgiven." ⁴⁹Those who were reclining *at the table* with Him began to say to themselves, "Who is this *man* who even forgives sins?" ⁵⁰And He

said to the woman, "Your faith has saved you; go in peace."

The woman had an appreciation for Jesus that Simon did not. She recognized the size of her debt and her need for forgiveness. It was her faith in Jesus' power to forgive that made the difference. Luke wants his readers to see the contrast between the woman and Simon, and to some extent between the woman and the other guests who are amazed at Jesus' claim that He can forgive sins.

If I were to ask the question, "As which kind of debtor did Simon see himself, a 50-denarius debtor or a 500-denarius debtor?" How would you answer? It is my contention that Simon saw himself as no debtor at all. He had no debt before God. He had earned his right standing before God and deserved it. He deserved Jesus' presence at his house. He owed God and Jesus nothing. The problem with Simon was not that he was bad. He was a good man. The problem was his inability to see his own sinfulness. Because he did not see his own sinfulness, he saw no need for a savior. The woman in our story recognized both her sin and her need for a savior. That is the point of the parable.

Why would Luke have chosen to record this parable? Unfortunately many of the folks of Jesus' day, like Simon, did not see themselves as debtors either. During the days of the early church, the Jews, the Judaizers in particular, saw themselves as law keepers who did it all, got it all right. They had no room for other folks who had lived lives of sin and at hearing the story of Jesus saw their sin. Those Gentiles came to Jesus, but the Judaizers contended they needed to get right by keeping the Law. It is easy to see something of the situation in Jesus' life and the situation in the life of Luke's church. The message seems rather clear. One needs to see himself as a sinner if he's going to appreciate the grace of God.

The question we posed as we began our study of this parable is a good one: "Is it better to be bad and then be good than to always be pretty good?" No, it is not better to be bad and then be good than to always be pretty good. What matters is that you see yourself as a sinner with a debt that cannot be paid by human effort. Both debtors in the parable have debts they could not repay and should have been terribly grateful when the master forgave that debt. Unfortunately those with large debts may see grace more clearly than those with small ones. Simon should have recognized his debt, and so should we.

When God reigns, I will appreciate God's grace and the forgiveness that I have. I will recognize my sin and my need for forgiveness that comes from God.

Parable of Unworthy Servants

In a society that emphasizes workers' rights, the parable of the farmer and his slave seems out of place. It teaches a vital lesson for the disciple. One is saved by the grace of God and nothing one does renders him worthy. This is an important lesson that Paul worked hard to teach. It, therefore, seems appropriate that Luke, who traveled with Paul, would preserve and record this parable.

Jesus has just called His disciples to make sure they do not cause others to stumble (Luke 17:1-2). They must forgive when their brother or sister repents (vv. 3-4). The disciples understand the difficulty that comes in having the forgiving spirit Jesus requires. They ask Him to increase their faith (v. 5).

Jesus informs that just a little faith can do wonderful things. They must simply exercise that faith (v. 6). Then almost as an aside Jesus gives the parable of the farmer and his slave. It seems from the context that the parable is designed to help the disciples keep their focus and not begin to think too highly of their deeds of faith.

LUKE 17:7-10

7"**Which of you, having a slave plowing or tending sheep, will say to him when he has come in from the field, 'Come immediately and sit down to eat'?** 8"**But will he not say to him, 'Prepare something for me to eat, and *properly* clothe yourself and serve me while I eat and drink; and afterward you may eat and drink'?** 9"**He does not thank the slave because he did the things which were commanded, does he?** 10"**So you too, when you do all the things which are commanded you, say, 'We are unworthy slaves; we have done *only* that which we ought to have done.'"**

The call in this chapter is for Jesus' disciples to be people of faith and to live lives of faith. The context of this parable seems cold and impersonal. The relationship portrayed is what was expected of a slave in the first century AD. The farmer is not very wealthy. He has only one slave. That slave is instructed to plow during the day and then to prepare supper upon returning home at night. For doing such tasks, the slave does not even receive a "Thank you."

Jesus frequently found it necessary to teach His disciples what it meant to be servants. They, like us, wanted to be the ones served. He had to help them to learn that they were not called to work in the kingdom for rewards. It is unfortunate, but we answer the question, "Would you work harder if you received a raise?" with a "Yes, indeed." No disciple can ever say, "God is indebted to me. He owes me a reward." Salvation is by the grace of God. We have earned nothing. We are all unworthy slaves. We have only done what we have been called to do. We can never pat ourselves on the back and say, "What good Christians we are."

LIVING IN GOD'S REIGN

1. How will understanding the size of my debt to God as a sinner affect my response to my brothers and sisters when they hurt me?
2. Respond to the question, "Is it better to be bad and then be good than to always be pretty good?"
3. Discuss the significance of the doctrine of grace in terms of how the believer should understand his good works.
4. Look up the word grace in a concordance. Read several of the passages where the word occurs and explain how this lesson may affect the way you read those verses.

Jesus paid it all — all to Him I owe — Sin has left a Crimson stain — He washed it white as snow —

CHAPTER 5

God's Invitation to
Join in His Reign

Being invited to share in a meal, has always been an indication of one's status and importance with the one hosting the meal. In the Bible the kingdom of God, His reign, is frequently portrayed as a feast, a special meal, with the guests dining with God Himself. Jesus uses this metaphor in His parables to portray this gracious gift of God for believers.

Parable of the Big Dinner

One parable indicating the gracious invitation of the Lord to join His kingdom is the parable of the big dinner in Luke 14. This parable occurs only in Luke's Gospel although there is a similar parable in Matthew, which we will examine next.

The narrative begins with Jesus eating a meal with one of the leaders of the Pharisees on a Sabbath (Luke 14:1). At the meal, a man with dropsy (likely something like congestive heart failure and lots of edema) stepped forward. The man was probably an ugly character, who would have been deemed unclean, from the wrong side of the tracks, and, therefore, not invited to the feast. Those gathered were anxious to see what Jesus would do since it was, after all, a Sabbath. Jesus healed the man and then defended His right to do so on a Sabbath.

At that point Jesus noticed that many of those who had been invited were jockeying for the best seats around the dinner table. He taught that folks should take a place of lesser importance and wait to be invited to take a better place rather than choosing the better place and be asked to move to a place indicating lesser status. To do otherwise would be terribly embarrassing. This also served as the call so typical of Jesus for His disciples to seek to serve rather than to be exalted. Jesus put it simply: "For everyone who exalts himself will be humbled, and he who humbles himself will be exalted" (Luke 14:11). People, Jesus said, should also invite others to meals who could not return the favor.

At this point in the story one of those at the feast made an assumption to which Jesus would respond and give the parable under consideration.

LUKE 14:15

When one of those who were reclining *at the table* with Him heard this, he said to Him, "Blessed is everyone who will eat bread in the kingdom of God!"

The man had heard what Jesus said, seen what Jesus did, and understood the kingdom of God as a feast like the one he was attending, something really desirable. He responds, "Blessed is everyone who eats in the kingdom of God." This man was saying, or at least thinking, "And that's us. We are the folks who will eat in the kingdom of God, who will enjoy this grand feast." It is in response to that statement that Jesus gives the following parable.

[16]But He said to him, "A man was giving a big dinner, and he invited many; [17]and at the dinner hour he sent his slave to say to those who had been invited, 'Come; for everything is ready now.' [18]"But they all alike began to make excuses. The first one said to him, 'I have bought a piece of land and I need to go out and look at it; please consider me excused.' [19]"Another one said, 'I have bought five yoke of oxen, and I am going to try them out; please consider me excused.' [20]"Another one said, 'I have married a wife, and for that reason I cannot come.' [21]"And the slave came *back* and reported this to his master. Then the head of the household became angry and said to his slave, 'Go out at once into the streets and lanes of the city and bring in here the poor and crippled and blind and lame.' [22]"And the slave said, 'Master, what you commanded has been done, and still there is room.' [23]"And the master said to the slave, 'Go out into the highways and along the hedges, and compel *them* to come in, so that my house may be filled. [24]"For I tell you, none of those men who were invited shall taste of my dinner.'"

Notice that those being invited are not getting a last-minute invitation. They had received an invitation earlier. It really is a second invitation to say, "The feast to which you were earlier invited and accepted is now ready. It is now time to come." The master sends his servants to all those who had RSVP'ed and are expected to attend. "Everything is now ready."

They all began to make excuses. The first one said, "I bought a piece of land and I need to go out and look at it. Please consider me excused." This is a very lame excuse. Imagine land in Palestine. Much of it is rocky, arid, and on the side of a mountain. One does not buy a piece of land in Palestine unless he has first looked at it. It may be in the desert. It may be in the middle of a wadi, a dry riverbed in the summer but the middle of a raging river during the rainy season. One would never buy a piece of land without first looking at it. This is a lame excuse. No one would do such a thing.

Another said, "I've bought five yoke of oxen. I must go to try them out. Please consider me excused." That would be like someone today saying, "I just bought a used car. I need to go test drive it." One does not buy a yoke of oxen without making sure that those animals will pull together. It just is not done.

The third excuse is perhaps the lamest of all, "I have married a wife and for this reason I cannot come." No good, self-respecting Jewish man would suggest that his wife keeps him from doing anything or that he could not be away from his wife long enough to do what he needs to do.

The slave came back and reported this to his master. Quite understandably, the head of the household became angry and said to his slave, "Go out into the streets and the lanes of the city and bring in here the poor and the crippled and the blind and the lame." After some time, the slave reports back, "Master what you have commanded has been done and there is still room." The slaves had initially gone to the streets and lanes, major thoroughfares, and invited folks. The master now says, "Go to the highways, along the hedges . . ." He is instructing them to move on to the back streets, the lesser traveled places. There they are to "compel them to come in so that my house may be filled, for I tell you none of these men who were invited shall taste my dinner."

Jesus has told a wonderful story. From the context of that story, it becomes clear that the invitation initially went out to people who should have come but who would say, "No." The connection is easy to make. The Jews, like those gathered at the meal where Jesus was, were people who had said "Yes" to God's invitation. After all, they were the chosen people. But ultimately, when it came to the lifestyle that Jesus demanded, they would say, "No." God would be forced to go to the highways. Finally He would even invite folks from the wrong side of the tracks. He would invite people that His audience would never dream could be a part of God's great party, His kingdom. God would open the door for tax collectors and sinners, the very people the religious leaders of Jesus' day disdained. Ultimately God would open the doors of His banquet hall even for those hated Gentiles. Those were folks for whom the religious people of Jesus' day, and perhaps the religious people even today, would never have room.

Parable of the Wedding Feast

In many ways the parable of the wedding feast in Matthew 22 parallels the parable of the big dinner. There are, however, some slight differences that provide some additional information about God's invitation.

The previous chapter ends with the chief priests and the Pharisees hearing Jesus' parables, and understanding that He was speaking about them. They begin their plot to seize Jesus, but, because of their fear of the people, because the people considered Jesus to be a prophet, they backed off. It is at this point that Jesus gives another parable. The parable clearly addresses the reaction of the religious of Jesus' day.

MATTHEW 22:1-14

[1]Jesus spoke to them again in parables, saying, [2]"The kingdom of heaven may be compared to a king who gave a wedding feast for his son. [3]"And he sent out his slaves to call those who had been invited to the wedding feast, and they were unwilling to come. [4]"Again he sent out other slaves saying, 'Tell those who have been invited, "Behold, I have prepared my dinner; my oxen and my fattened livestock are *all* butchered and everything is ready; come to the wedding feast."' [5]"But they paid no attention and went their way, one to his own farm, another to his business, [6]and the rest seized his slaves and mistreated them and killed them. [7]"But the king was enraged, and he sent his armies and destroyed those murderers and set their city on fire. [8]"Then he said to his slaves, 'The wedding is ready, but those who were invited were not worthy. [9]"Go therefore to the main highways, and as many as you find *there*, invite to the wedding feast.' [10]"Those slaves went out into the streets and gathered together all they found, both evil and good; and the wedding hall was filled with dinner guests.

[11]"But when the king came in to look over the dinner guests, he saw a man there who was not dressed in wedding clothes, [12]and he said to him, 'Friend, how did you come in here without wedding clothes?' And the man was speechless. [13]"Then the king said to the servants, 'Bind him hand and foot, and throw him into the outer darkness; in that place there will be weeping and gnashing of teeth.' [14]"For many are called, but few *are* chosen."

This time the meal is a royal wedding feast, a very grand time. Everyone who came was treated royally. The invitations were reserved for the privileged few. They came in the door, their heads would be anointed with special per-fumed oil, and their feet washed. They were given a brand new garment.

The king sent out his slaves to call those who had been invited. Notice again that the invitation had gone out earlier. Again those invited were unwill-ing to come. He again sent out his slaves saying, "Tell those who have been invited, 'Behold I have prepared my dinner, my oxen and my fatted livestock are all butchered, everything is ready. Come to the wedding feast.'" The king has actually given them a second chance to come. But the privileged citizens of his land paid no attention to the call from their king. They all went their way, one to his farm and another to his business. Notice they are too busy with their own affairs to come. The average Jew would not have had meat with his meals on normal days. The fatted livestock were reserved for very special occa-sions. Despite the fact that this is an occasion to be with the king and to dine with him, the citizens refuse to come.

At this point some of the citizens did the unimaginable. They seized the king's slaves and mistreated them. This provides a second tier or prong to the parable. The parable has at least two main points. It is no surprise that the king was enraged. He sent his armies and destroyed those murderers and set their city on fire.

Then the king said to the slaves, "The wedding feast is ready. Those who were invited are not worthy. Go therefore to the main highways, as many as you find there invite them in to the feast." The slaves followed their master's instructions and went into the streets gathering together all they found, both evil and good, those from the wrong side of the tracks and those from the right side of the tracks. The wedding hall was filled with dinner guests.

Again the parable takes a strange turn. The king came in to look over the dinner guests, and he saw a man who was there but not dressed in wedding clothes. I always felt a little sorry for the fellow who had come but does not have a wedding garment. I thought perhaps he could not afford the tuxedo the event required. But the point is the garment was furnished. The man had refused to put on the garment. In so doing he had insulted the king and all those attending the feast. The king said to him, "Friend, how did you come in here without wedding clothes?" The man was speechless. He has no excuse. And the king said to his servants, "Bind him hand and foot and throw him into outer darkness. In that place there will be weeping and gnashing of teeth." The man is kicked out of the hall to a place where people will be in misery, from a place of great joy to a place of mourning.

The text ends with, "For many are called but few are chosen." This short verse provides a wonderful insight into the question of election, predestina-tion, and the atonement. Notice in the parable that the invitation ultimately goes out to everyone, even the unexpected. Entering the wedding feast is an opportunity available to all. The word "chosen" is the same word sometimes translated "elect." "Many are called, few are chosen." Who in the parable are the "called" or the "invited"? The invitation originally went out to a select few (in the context Jews), but before the parable ends everyone is invited. Who in Jesus' parable are the chosen people? The chosen people are those who come to the feast and who put on the wedding garments. And so, who are God's chosen people? Who are God's elect? The elect are those who have elected to be the elect. They have chosen to attend the feast; they have accepted the invitation. The chosen are those who respond as they ought. It is not as though God has made an arbitrary choice. God has chosen all of those who respond favorably to His invitation in Jesus.

What did Jesus intend for His audience to learn from this parable? He was addressing people who saw themselves as privileged but whose lives failed to live up to God's intention for them. He was teaching them that a lot of people who have said they are going to the wedding feast will not be there because they are saying "No" to Him. Some will refuse the invitation by making excuses. Others will say no in a much more negative way, rebelling against God and His messengers. Jesus says that their city is going to be destroyed.

There will be those, however, who respond as they ought. They will accept the message of Jesus and come to the feast. There is still a danger yet lurking even for those disciples. Saying "Yes" to Jesus is not enough. There may be one who does not put on the wedding garment. He says "Yes," but he does not live like folks who say "Yes" should live. Jesus' teaching about the wedding garment parallels the words of Paul: "Only conduct yourselves in a manner worthy of the gospel of Christ. . . ." (Phil. 1:27). Putting on the wedding garment is living like a saved person. It is possible to come to the feast but miss the point.

It is easy to understand how the parable would apply to Jesus' audience, to those Pharisees who are critical of Him, who think they have received the invitation, who receive it first but who will not respond favorably to Jesus, some of whom will respond in a negative and violent way. Matthew would have chosen this parable for his Gospel because of His intended message for His audience. Matthew's intended audience would be the Judaizers of his day, the Jews who contended one must keep the law, those to whom the promise initially went out but had no room for Gentiles. The Gentiles who read Matthew's account would see themselves as the folks from the wrong side of the tracks, the outsiders who will say "Yes." Early disciples would also grasp the significance of putting on the wedding garment, living that life of "Yes."

The message for today's reader is also clear. A lot of religious folks are not really going to respond as they ought. They miss the point.

Parable of the Barren Fig Tree

The last parable in this unit is the parable of the barren fig tree in Luke 13. While still dealing with God's invitation, His call, this parable shifts to emphasize repentance and its place in the call. The narrative surrounding the parable begins with a question from Jesus' audience.

LUKE 13:1-5

¹**Now on the same occasion there were some present who reported to Him about the Galileans whose blood Pilate had mixed with their sacrifices. ²And Jesus said to them, "Do you suppose that these Galileans were *greater* sinners than all *other* Galileans because they suffered this *fate*? ³"I tell you, no, but unless you repent, you will all likewise perish. ⁴"Or do you suppose that those eighteen on whom the tower in Siloam fell and killed them were *worse* culprits than all the men who live in Jerusalem? ⁵"I tell you, no, but unless you repent, you will all likewise perish."**

The same occasion is the parable Jesus had just taught about being ready for His return. Some of those in His audience reported a time when Pilate killed some Galileans who had come to make their sacrifice, mingling their blood with the blood of their sacrifices perhaps in the temple in the Court of the Gentiles. We cannot be certain as to the exact incident these people had in mind. The social tension of the period made revolutionary activity in those days possible at any time. Pilate found himself as governor of a troubled province far from Rome. His situation was precarious, and so he frequently acted to put down possible rebellion. Josephus says that Galileans were especially susceptible to revolt.[12] Any attack against Jews who had come to offer sacrifices was horrendous whatever its reason.

Jesus refuses to attribute the cause for the tragedy to some sin these men had committed as the Jews did (cf. John 9:1-3). On the contrary, He affirms the sinfulness of all people. "Are they worse than other folks?" He asks. "No, but if you don't repent, you'll be worse off than they are."

"Or do you suppose those eighteen on whom the tower in Siloam fell and killed them were worse culprits than all the men who live in Jerusalem." Again, we are uncertain which tower Jesus has in mind. It would seem to be a tower that is part of an aqueduct to bring water to Jerusalem. The word "siloam"

---

[12] *Life*, 92. 17.

means sent and also serves as the name of a pool in Jerusalem at the end of
Hezekiah's tunnel (John 9:7). In a construction accident, the tower fell and
killed eighteen of the workers. Because bad things happened to them, does
that make them necessarily bad? Bad things happen to Galileans. Are they
worse than other folks? Bad things happened to these construction workers.
Are they worse than other folks who live in Jerusalem? The Jews of Jesus' day
may well have responded, "Yes!" They had assumed that bad things happened
to bad people, much as Job's supposed friends assumed. Jesus responds, "I tell
you no, unless you repent, you will all likewise perish."

The question opens the door for Jesus to talk about the message of repentance. Repentance was at the heart of John's preaching (Matt. 3:2) and at the
heart of Jesus' preaching (Matt. 4:17). The word "repent"[13] in Greek literally
means "to change one's mind." The background is the Hebrew word translated "repent" (*shuv*). That word means to turn, to change directions. One is
headed in one direction; he turns to go another. The call to repent is a call to
change one's direction in life.

Jesus tells the following parable as a call to repent.

LUKE 13:6-9

⁶**And He *began* telling this parable: "A man had a fig tree
which had been planted in his vineyard; and he came looking for
fruit on it and did not find any. ⁷"And he said to the vineyard-
keeper, 'Behold, for three years I have come looking for fruit on
this fig tree without finding any. Cut it down! Why does it even
use up the ground?' ⁸"And he answered and said to him, 'Let it
alone, sir, for this year too, until I dig around it and put in fertil-
izer; ⁹and if it bears fruit next year, *fine*; but if not, cut it down.'"**

The owner of the vineyard had planted a fig tree in the middle of his vineyard.
At the appropriate time he came looking for fruit on it, but he did not find any. He
told the vineyard keeper that his patience had worn thin. For three years he had
come looking for fruit on this fig tree but found none. So he gave the vineyard
keeper these instructions, "Cut it down. Why does it even use up the ground?"
And the worker responded, "Give it one more chance, sir. This year I will dig
around it and fertilize it. If it bears fruit next year, fine. If it does not, cut it down."

The fig tree in our story is a privileged fig tree. This fig tree is planted in
a vineyard, a place where there would be lots of tilling, perhaps even irrigation,
and fertilization. That simply is not the norm in an orchard. This tree has

---

[13] *Metanoieō* (μετανοιέω).

everything going for it. In Palestine, folks do not plant trees just for the shade. Unless it bears fruit, it is useless and wastes good land. On the third year, a fig tree should be bearing fruit. The text may well suggest that the man has come now for three years looking for fruit, perhaps years four, five and six. Yet there is no fruit. This privileged tree, with everything going for it has no fruit. It is using up good ground and is an insult to its situation.

The worker asks for a reprieve, a second chance. From the text it is clear that Jesus is the last chance for the Jewish people to respond to the grace of God. They are favored people. These Jews in Jesus' audience who are asking about others, and thinking surely those who died were in need of repentance, need to understand that all people need to repent. Just because they are a favored people does not mean they are exempt from this need. They have many wonderful opportunities, but, unless they repent, the end is near. Jesus is their last opportunity.

Notice, we have established the meaning of this parable in the context of Jesus' audience in Luke's Gospel. The same applies to Luke's own audience, for the church in his day. The church has heard the story of Jesus. They have responded by professing faith in Jesus. If they do not respond favorably to the story of Jesus with changed lives, there is no place for them to turn. They are now the privileged ones.

The same message rings true today. Many have heard that story over and over again. Jesus is their last chance.

LIVING IN GOD'S REIGN

1. Discuss the kind of "lame excuses" people sometimes give today for not responding to the gospel.
2. Seeing oneself as privileged can either cause pride or humility. Discuss how and why this is the case.
3. Discuss how the person who responded favorably to the invitation to the wedding feast but was not wearing the wedding garment might apply today.
4. Discuss the following statement, "Privilege means responsibility," as it applies to this lesson.

CHAPTER 6
When God Reigns,
There Will Be Joy

Imagine that it is 1947 and you are a young man who is watching his goats. One of your goats wanders off apparently into one of the caves on a distant hill. You pick up a rock. You heave it into the cave and . . . crash! . . . you break a jar. You go inside to look around and sure enough, inside that jar there were manuscripts, manuscripts that date from 100 BC. You have found a treasure! Would you be excited? Of course, all of us would. What a wonderful, exciting thing to do.

You're a fellow in Suffolk, England. You have been plowing along, and, as you plow, you hit a box. You bend down and dig around the box. You open the box, and in it you find gold and silver and pewter dishes from the Roman era. Would you be excited? Of course anyone would.

You are diving off the coast of Florida. You find a sunken ship and in it doubloons, lots of Spanish coins worth a lot of money. What a wonderful treasure! Would you be excited? Of course you would.

You're a fifty-five-year-old widow and your husband is a little older than you are. He has emphysema. He is a truck driver but is currently on disability. You simply cannot survive on his disability compensation long. You may lose you house. You are worried about how you will be able to pay the bills. There is a knock on the door. The fellow who is at the door says, "Here's an envelope; it contains a check for one million dollars. You have just won the *Reader's Digest* Sweepstakes! You will receive nine million dollars more over the next twenty years!" Would you be excited? Of course you would!

We're always excited by stories of treasure. I think Jesus knew that very well, and so our next two parables are about wonderful treasures, about what God has done to bring a treasure to His people.

Parable of the Hidden Treasure

This unit examines parables that deal with the joy that comes when God is reigning in the lives of believers. It would seem that Jesus is concerned that His disciples will have a misunderstanding of the nature of the kingdom. They may be tempted to see the kingdom as primarily a group of rules, things that are demanded of the believer. They may fail to see the kingdom as a wonderful privilege that fills the lives of believers with joy. The two parables in this unit (Matt. 13:44-46) are what I call "sister parables," parables given often in the same historical context to teach one central message. Each of these parables, the parable of the hidden treasure and the parable of the pearl of great price, is but one sentence long, three verses in total.

In the first chapter we referred to a statement made by Frederick Borsch. He says that the parables of Jesus ". . . designed to lure the hearers to become participants. They are invited to play parts . . . ."[14] Jesus knows how much we dream of treasures and finding treasures and receiving treasures. He tells two treasure stories. And in each parable we step forward to play the part of the person who finds the treasure.

The first parable is the parable of the hidden treasure. We are not sure whether Jesus told these two parables together or whether Matthew grouped the two parables to make an emphatic point. On the surface it seems likely that Jesus told the parables so He could reinforce His message: two parables, even in a row, to drive home the message. These parables in Matthew's Gospel are told only to the disciples. The disciples are now by themselves. It would seem that they are told by Jesus to help the disciples see the value of becoming disciples, so that they do not begin to view being a disciple as an onerous task, but rather as a wonderful one.

MATTHEW 13:44

⁴⁴"The kingdom of heaven is like a treasure hidden in the field, which a man found and hid *again*; and from joy over it he goes and sells all that he has and buys that field."

It was not at all unusual in the first century AD for someone to hide money in a field. The rabbis in Jesus' day had a saying: "There is only one safe repository for money—the earth." One could hide his money in his house, but, when marauders would come through, one might get driven out of his house, and the marauders would take that money. One could invest the money, but he

---

[14] Frederick Houk Borsch, *Many Things in Parables: Extravagant Stories of the New Community* (Philadelphia: Fortress, 1988), p. 1.

might lose it. The safe place was a hole in the ground. All sorts of "mayonnaise jars" have been found in digs in Palestine where people have hidden their money in the backyard. Someone in our story has done just that. The man in our story is a sharecropper. He has been farming his rented field. As he plowed the ground, he hits something, a box full of money. He digs a hole, buries it again, goes, takes all that he has, and buys the field so that the field will be his.

One may be tempted to ask some natural questions that may send the reader the wrong direction and cause him to misunderstand the parable. One may be tempted to emphasize those questions and miss the real point of the parable. One is tempted to ask, "Is this legal?" Is it legal for him to buy the field so that the treasure will be his? "Is the rule of the day 'finders keepers, losers weepers'?" "Is this really ethical?" "Should he tell the landowner?" "Should he and the owner of the land split the money?" "Is it really fair?" In our exegesis of this parable, we will not really answer those questions at all.

Parable of the Pearl of Great Price

The second parable is the pearl of great price. This time two verses but again just one sentence.

MATTHEW 13:45-46

[45]"Again, the kingdom of heaven is like a merchant seeking fine pearls, [46]and upon finding one pearl of great value, he went and sold all that he had and bought it."

This time the kingdom of heaven is likened to a merchant seeking fine pearls. Upon finding one pearl of great price, he went and sold all that he had and bought it. In the first century AD, merchants traveled all over the world looking for great pearls to the Indian Ocean, the Black Sea, the Mediterranean—wherever they might find pearls. Cleopatra is supposed to have had one pearl valued at approximately two million dollars in spending money today. There was a fascination with pearls and their beauty. The man in our story is called a merchant. The word seems to refer to a wholesaler. It is the word from which we get our English word emporium. This man buys pearls and then sells them to others who make jewelry out of them. He has spent his whole life looking for these wonderful pearls. He finds the prettiest one that he has ever seen in his whole life. He sells all that he has and invests everything that he has in this single wonderful pearl that he intends to keep his whole life long.

Again, one can overflow with some natural questions. "How's this guy going to make a living from now on?" "Has he not invested everything he has in this pearl?" "Is he not being foolish?" He will never be able to buy any other pearls to sell them to make a living. "Is he not facing financial disaster; is he not in real trouble?"

There is a story among the rabbis that I think illustrates the same point Jesus is trying to make with the disciples.

> Rabbi Jochanan was going up from Tiberias to Sepphoris and he was leaning on the shoulder of Rabbi Chijjah ben Abbah. They came to a field plot, and he said, "This used to belong to me, but I sold it that I might study the Law." They came to a field of olives, and he said, ""This used to belong to me, but I sold it that I might study the Law." Rabbi Chijjah ben Abbah began to weep. When he was asked why, he said "I weep because you have nothing for your old age." Rabbi Jochanan answered, "Chijjah, my son, is it a small thing in your eyes that I sold something that was created in six days that in its place I might gain that which was given in forty days and forty nights?"

Rabbi Jochanan saw the value in things determined by how long it took God to create them. It took forty days and forty nights to give the law and only six days to create the universe and all it contains. Surely the law should be seen as more valuable. More important than Jochanan's way of discovering relative value was his realization of that value and how that realization then affected his life. He had given up all his physical possessions so that he could have the law in his heart, so that he could study and understand the law. So, as far as he was concerned, he really had not given up anything. What he received was worth far more than what he gave up.

I illustrate the story among my students at Lipscomb University as follows. You are in the student center, and you are met by a man who says, "I have a deal for you. Here's my deal. I'll give you one million dollars for all your earthly possessions. You must give me your car. You owe more on it than it's worth. Give me your clothes—you're tired of those anyway; they are out of style. Give me those CD's—you can go buy some more. Give me your books—you haven't really used them this semester anyhow. Give me all the stuff you have, and I'll give you one million dollars. Is it a deal?" I have yet to find a single student who would say no to such an offer. What they would give up is not at all worth what they would receive.

Perhaps no one in the Bible understood this better than the Apostle Paul. In Philippians chapter 3, Paul has been talking about those who are Judaizers, about those he terms the "false circumcision" who have misunderstood the real significance of circumcision and are boasting about their Jewish heritage.

PHILIPPIANS 3:4-11

 . . . [4]although I myself might have confidence even in the flesh. If anyone else has a mind to put confidence in the flesh, I far more: [5]circumcised the eighth day, of the nation of Israel, of the tribe of Benjamin, a Hebrew of Hebrews; as to the Law, a Pharisee; [6]as to zeal, a persecutor of the church; as to the righteousness which is in the Law, found blameless. [7]But whatever things were gain to me, those things I have counted as loss for the sake of Christ. [8]More than that, I count all things to be loss in view of the surpassing value of knowing Christ Jesus my Lord, for whom I have suffered the loss of all things, and count them but rubbish so that I may gain Christ, [9]and may be found in Him, not having a righteousness of my own derived from *the* Law, but that which is through faith in Christ, the righteousness which *comes* from God on the basis of faith, [10]that I may know Him and the power of His resurrection and the fellowship of His sufferings, being conformed to His death; [11]in order that I may attain to the resurrection from the dead.

Paul tells the Philippians that he will boast with Judaizers item for item. He was circumcised on the eighth day, that is, born a Jew, reared a Jew from the very beginning. He had that ideal start. He was "of the nation of Israel," not some sort of proselyte. He was "of the tribe of Benjamin," a tribe known for its loyalty. After all the first king of Israel came from that tribe, and he, Paul, originally named Saul, was named after that king. His people were folks known for their loyalty and known to be fierce fighters. He was "a Hebrew of Hebrews," likely indicating that he was a Hebrew-speaking Hebrew since many Jews in the first century AD no longer spoke their native tongue. In addition to all those wonderful parts of his heritage, Paul proclaimed himself to be "as to the law, a Pharisee," the strictest sect of them all. In addition Paul says that "as to zeal" he was "a persecutor of the church." He took his faith seriously enough to persecute those whom he thought opposed it. When it comes to "righteousness which is in the law," Paul says he was found blameless.

 Despite this wonderful heritage, Paul said he learned an important lesson. "But whatever things were gain to me, those things I counted as lost for the sake of Christ." You see Paul was a man on the way up in the Jewish world; he had the equivalent of a Ph.D. in Religion in his day; he was a great rabbi in training at the time of the stoning of Stephen. He had everything. He lost his status and perhaps his family's wealth when he became a Christian. Paul declared everything to be loss in view of the surpassing value of knowing

Christ Jesus. He had come to know what really matters. He had found the great treasure, the pearl of great price. He considers everything else that he once valued as rubbish, the garbage pile, the manure heap, in comparison to knowing Jesus and gaining a righteousness that is not derived from the law or personal merit but comes through faith in Christ. For Paul, what he gave up did not really matter. It was the garbage pile, the manure heap. What he gained, knowing Jesus, knowing the power of His resurrection, ah, that was a wonderful treasure! He had found the treasure. He had found real joy. He gave up everything to get that treasure, but he really gave up nothing.

That, I think, is the point of the two parables in Matthew 13. These parables are not about gambling because the people in the parables are not gambling anything. They are not risking anything. They are not even playing the stock market because they know what they will receive at the very beginning. One man knows that he will ultimately have the field and the treasure in that field, and the other man knows he will have that pearl, the one he has always wanted.

In a way, the parables are about sacrifice. But really there is no sacrifice at all because two men in the parables are getting something that they value more than what they are giving up. They give up all their possessions to get this wonderful treasure.

The parables are about a kind of urgency, a rashness. Notice both men act immediately. Immediately one goes out and sells all that he has to buy the field. Immediately the other goes out and sells all that he has to get the pearl of great price. For both men it is a now or never proposition. They cannot let this opportunity pass by. In a way the parables are about risk, and yet there is no risk because they know that they will receive the treasure.

The Christian faith, the kingdom, is an adventure and a treasure. Jesus wants His audience to see that. Being a disciple of Jesus is not just a bunch of dumb rules. You do have to do what Jesus says. You must take up His cross daily and follow Him. But that is not dismal and miserable. One must see the treasure and make living the life a joy. It is not about drudgery at all. It is joy. Jesus is trying to help His disciples, the twelve guys, see the Christian life in this new fresh way. Matthew writes a kind of handbook for early Christians, this Gospel, to help the disciples in his era see what it means to be a Christian in an alien world. He wants them to learn from these parables that Christianity is a joy. That is the message for believers in the twenty-first century as well. One can try to get folks to live the Christian life by threatening them with hell. That may work to some degree for a little while, but, if one hopes to change people, he must help them appreciate the joy of being a Christian. That makes a difference.

LIVING IN GOD'S REIGN

1. It has been said that fear is not a good long-term motivator. Rather than "hell-fire-and-brimstone" sermons, how can we better motivate Christians to live the Christian life?

2. How does an appreciation of the kingdom as a treasure affect the way Christians are involved in evangelism?

3. What are the forces at work that tend to make Christians view the Christian life as something other than joy and a treasure?

4. How could these two parables affect the lives of the twelve, the life of Matthew's church, and the church today?

CHAPTER 7

When God Reigns, I'll Care About Others

Over and over again in the Bible, the reader learns that relationship with God affects relationships with others. When asked, "What is the greatest commandment?" (Matt. 22:36), Jesus responded in the way the great rabbis before Him had: "'You shall love the Lord your God with all your heart, and with all your soul, and with all your mind.' This is the great and foremost commandment. The second is like it, 'You shall love your neighbor as yourself.'" In this chapter we will examine parables in which Jesus shows His audience how God's reign in their lives will affect their relationships with other people.

Parable of the Lost Sheep

Three "sister" parables are grouped together in Luke chapter 15. Although the first parable, the parable of the lost sheep, appears independently in Matthew's Gospel (Matt. 18:12-14) in a setting where Jesus is teaching the twelve the need for bringing back the erring, in Luke it appears as the first of three lost parables. Since the context in Matthew is different from the one in Luke, Jesus may well have used the same parable on different occasions with different audiences. It is not necessary that the evangelist concocted one of the settings.

It is unfortunate, but often the connectedness between all three parables in Luke's Gospel is lost. Frequently the preacher and the student of Luke will deal with only the first half of the third parable.

Luke gives the context for the three parables in 15:1-2:

> **¹Now all the tax collectors and the sinners were coming near Him to listen to Him. ²Both the Pharisees and the scribes *began* to grumble, saying, "This man receives sinners and eats with them."**

The complaint of the Pharisees and scribes regarding the fact that Jesus would eat with tax collectors and sinners led to these parables. It is significant that Jesus' audience would have been composed of two diverse groups of people—Pharisees and scribes, and tax collectors and sinners. That Jesus would design parables that would have a message for both of these groups should not be surprising.

LUKE 15:3-6

³So He told them this parable, saying, "'What man among you, if he has a hundred sheep and has lost one of them, does not leave the ninety-nine in the open pasture and go after the one which is lost until he finds it? ⁵"When he has found it, he lays it on his shoulders, rejoicing. ⁶"And when he comes home, he calls together his friends and his neighbors, saying to them, 'Rejoice with me, for I have found my sheep which was lost!'"

The man in this parable had an average size flock for the first century AD. He had lost one sheep. Typically shepherds would begin the morning by picking up a rock for each of his sheep as they left the fold. Periodically during the day, he would count his sheep by laying down the rocks. If at any time he had more rocks left in his hands than sheep, he would recognize he had lost one or more of his sheep.

This author has always been interested in the fact that of all the animals God could have chosen to illustrate His people, He chose sheep. Sheep are some of the dumbest animals one could ever find. They are near-sighted, easily get lost, and apparently have no sense of direction to find their way home. They cannot swim, and so rapid-moving water frightens them. That indicates, by the way, the importance of "He leads me beside still waters . . ." in Psalm 23. They are not like Lassie in all of the movies and television programs. When Lassie is separated from her family on a trip to New York, she finds her way back to California again. That is not the case with sheep. They just get more lost. They are not particularly bright. They do not seek shelter to have their young, but will give birth wherever they are. God chooses sheep to illustrate His people—near-sighted, easily lost, in need of a shepherd.

One of the sheep wanders off. The shepherd goes to find it. When he finds it, he places it on his shoulders and goes home. There he gathers his friends and his neighbors saying, "Rejoice with me for I have found my sheep which was lost." He is excited because he has found that one lost sheep.

Jesus goes on to explain the significance of His parable:

LUKE 15:7

[7]"I tell you that in the same way, there will be *more* joy in heaven over one sinner who repents than over ninety-nine righteous persons who need no repentance."

There is the same kind of excitement in heaven when a lost one is found. God and His angels are thrilled when the sinner returns.

There is a real danger in attempts to allegorize these parables. Some want to emphasize that the sheep wandered astray on its own, thus making differences between the sheep and the coin in the parable that follows. It would seem that such an approach presses the text too far and may miss the reason Jesus may have told the parables on the same occasion and the reason Luke may have grouped them as he has done. Another allegorical interpretation suggests that these three parables are about the trinity. In the first we meet God, the Good Shepherd, that is, God the Son; in the second we meet God the Holy Spirit; and, of course, since the third parable has a father and a lost son, we meet God the Father. Again, such an interpretation is pressing the text beyond what the immediate context seems to indicate as the message.

There is also real danger that one may misread the statement of Jesus in verse 7 about "righteous persons who need no repentance." One might assume that Jesus was saying that scribes and Pharisees had no need of repentance. From the context of the Gospels, we know that is not true. Jesus said earlier, "*It is* not those who are well who need a physician, but those who are sick. I have not come to call the righteous but sinners to repentance" (Luke 5:31-32; cf. Matt. 9:12). One might assume that Jesus was saying that the Pharisees, the scribes, the religious leaders of the day, were well folks, the righteous. They at least saw themselves as righteous, needing no repentance.

The message of this parable is rather simple. God cares about the lost. The situation in Jesus' life that brought about the parable was the question of the Pharisees and scribes, "Why are you eating with these publicans and sinners? Why are you eating with these terrible folks, these outsiders, these folks who are not ceremonially clean?" Jesus' response is, "because God cares about the lost." There's joy in heaven over one sinner who repents.

Parable of the Lost Coin

LUKE 15:8-10

[8]"Or what woman, if she has ten silver coins and loses one coin, does not light a lamp and sweep the house and search carefully until she finds it? [9]"When she has found it, she calls together her friends and neighbors, saying, 'Rejoice with me, for I have found the coin

which I had lost!' [10]"In the same way, I tell you, there is joy in the
presence of the angels of God over one sinner who repents."

The woman in this parable had ten silver coins. The Greek word here for
coins is *drachmas*. A drachma was equal to a denarius. The word drachma is
the Greek name for a coin, denarius really the Latin name for the coin, each
representing minimum wage for a day's labor.

There are all sorts of assumptions about what this collection of coins she
had might have been. Perhaps it was her household budget. Women in the first
century AD often managed the household budget. It would then represent the
money to buy groceries, take care of household needs, etc. The other possibil-
ity that some have suggested is that the coins might well have been her dowry.
Part of her dowry would have remained with her so that if her husband ever
died or left her she would have something to take care of her. Her father would
have tried to guarantee her well-being. The woman then would have lost one
coin out of her dowry. There was apparently a tradition in the first century AD
that, if one lost one of those coins, for every coin one lost, one's husband would
be unfaithful that many times. So, perhaps this is a part of the story.

Whatever the case is, the woman has lost her coin. Again, the real danger
is that we may misunderstand the significance of this. The coin represents minimum wage for a day's labor. Minimum wage for a day today is about $42.00.
She has thus lost a pretty good sum for a poor lady. Notes in some older translations make it sound like she has lost sixteen or seventeen cents. I always tell
my students at Lipscomb, I doubt they would scour their dorm rooms for sixteen or seventeen cents that they might have lost, but let them lose two twen-
ty-dollar bills and see how diligent a search they would conduct. The woman
lights a lamp and sweeps the house. She searches carefully until she finds it,
and when she has found it, she calls together her friends and neighbors saying, "Rejoice with me. I have found my coin which was lost." It sounds as if
she might be giving a party to celebrate her found coin.

Verse 10 provides a conclusion to this parable very much like verse 7 did
for the last parable: "In the same way I tell you there is joy in the presence of
the angels of God over one sinner who repents." The parables are clearly connected. The message is the same. God cares about the lost. His angels rejoice
when there is this one brought back again.

Parable of the Prodigal Son or the Lost Son(s)

If one looks up the word "prodigal" in an English dictionary, he will find
the following primary definition: "wasteful, spendthrift." One might, however,
find a secondary definition: "one who leaves and returns." In reality, that sec-

ondary definition comes from this parable. When we speak today of someone being a "prodigal son," we often do so not because the person being described fits the original meaning of the word, "wasteful, spendthrift," but because that person has left family and priorities and has now returned. This serves as a wonderful illustration of how Jesus' parables have affected the English language.

LUKE 15:11-24

[11]And He said, "A man had two sons. [12]"The younger of them said to his father, 'Father, give me the share of the estate that falls to me.' So he divided his wealth between them. [13]"And not many days later, the younger son gathered everything together and went on a journey into a distant country, and there he squandered his estate with loose living. [14]"Now when he had spent everything, a severe famine occurred in that country, and he began to be impoverished. [15]"So he went and hired himself out to one of the citizens of that country, and he sent him into his fields to feed swine. [16]"And he would have gladly filled his stomach with the pods that the swine were eating, and no one was giving *anything* to him. [17]"But when he came to his senses, he said, 'How many of my father's hired men have more than enough bread, but I am dying here with hunger! [18]I will get up and go to my father, and will say to him, "Father, I have sinned against heaven, and in your sight; [19]I am no longer worthy to be called your son; make me as one of your hired men."' [20]"So he got up and came to his father. But while he was still a long way off, his father saw him and felt compassion *for him*, and ran and embraced him and kissed him. [21]"And the son said to him, 'Father, I have sinned against heaven and in your sight; I am no longer worthy to be called your son.' [22]"But the father said to his slaves, 'Quickly bring out the best robe and put it on him, and put a ring on his hand and sandals on his feet; [23]and bring the fattened calf, kill it, and let us eat and celebrate; [24]for this son of mine was dead and has come to life again; he was lost and has been found.' And they began to celebrate."

Notice, the man in this parable had two sons. The normal inheritance laws would provide the older son with a double portion; the younger son would receive a single portion. He would have received one third of his father's wealth, normally at his father's death. Basically, the son says, "I don't want to wait until you die because then I'll be too old to enjoy my inheritance. Give it to me now." No matter how much of an insult this is to his father and how foolish it is, the father agrees and allows the son to have his way. Off he goes into a distant country. Why a distant country? Well, first of all, only a pagan land will work in this story; he could never care for pigs if he stayed in his homeland, Palestine. Perhaps Jesus is simply following what one would expect from a young man who wants to leave behind his old life and the standards of his father. When one runs away from home, one can do what one wants, there is no one standing over him to watch his deeds. Many a college student, when away from home and parents, wastes money and lives a sinful life.

The young man in the parable squanders his estate, all of his money, with loose living. The King James translation says "profligate living." The word is literally "unsaved living," living like an unsaved person. When he had spent everything, a severe famine occurred. One can always find what he wants, even during a famine, as long as he has money. When the money is gone, so are his new-found "friends." He began to be impoverished and so he hired himself out to one of the citizens of the country. His new employer sent him into the fields to feed swine. One needs to understand how serious a move this is for this young man. Feeding pigs was not only a dirty, smelly job, but feeding swine, unclean animals, would render a Jewish young man unclean. Being unclean would make it impossible for him to offer sacrifice and find forgiveness. It would make it impossible for him to associate with good people. This was the worst job one could imagine for a Jew.

Jesus informs His listeners that the young man would gladly have filled his stomach with the pods the swine were eating, but no one was giving anything to him. The word for "pods" here refers to carob. Carob beans resembled the pods on a Catalpa tree, beans inside a long pod. The pigs would eat these beans by popping the pods apart and eating the beans. Most people today recognize carob as "fake chocolate." This young man is tempted to eat what really is inedible.

This young man finally came to his senses. He reasoned, "Those hired hands who work for my father have more than enough bread to eat. Here I am dying here with hunger. I will get up, and I will go to my father, and I will say. . . ." It seems that at this point he is rehearsing his speech. He would tell his father that he now recognized he had sinned against heaven and against his father. He was no longer worthy to be considered a son. He simply wanted to serve his father as a slave. He recognized that he did not deserve being a son. He had insulted his father by his behavior and wasted his wealth. He would be so much better off as his father's slave than he was now in this foreign land.

So the young man got up and headed home to his father. While he was still afar off, his father saw him approaching. One wonders if he had been expecting and even longing for his return, always keeping a hopeful eye on the road. He felt compassion for his son, ran, embraced him, and kissed him. Running for an older man in the first century AD would have been unheard-of. It would have been deemed below the dignity of someone with status. The fact that the father ran shows how much he cared about his son. He embraced him. He kissed him.

It seems the son began his rehearsed speech: "Father, I have sinned against heaven and in your sight. I am no longer worthy to be called your son." Notice he does not get to finish the speech. The rest of the speech would have been, "I am no longer worthy to be called your son; make me as one of your hired men." His father interrupts him and instructs his slaves, "Quickly bring out the best robe and put it on him." The son is back in the family again. The best robe was reserved for members of the family for festive occasions. "Put a ring on his finger." The ring was likely here the signet ring used by the father to indicate his signature on bills of transaction. It would be like someone saying today, "Give him the family MasterCard" so that he can charge and be a part of the family. "Put sandals on his feet." Only slaves walk around barefooted. "Bring the fatted calf and kill it. Let us have a feast and celebrate. For this son of mine was dead and is alive; he was lost and is found." So they began to celebrate. The fatted calf was reserved for special occasions. Meat in the first century AD was not something that one enjoyed at every meal. It was rather unusual, and so this was a very special time.

Having heard Jesus deliver the first two parables in this chapter, His audience likely expected the story to end. One would likely expect Jesus to end by saying, "There'll be more rejoicing in heaven over one who returns than..." or "There will be great rejoicing when a sinner repents..." Clearly a sinner has repented, and the father is happy, as the shepherd was happy to find his lost sheep and the woman to find her lost coin. The father rejoiced to find his lost son.

We typically call this story the parable of the prodigal son, but in reality we ought to call it the parable of the lost son, or maybe better even yet, the parable of the lost sons. In reality two sons are lost but for different reasons. One runs away; the other stays, but he does not appreciate what he has.

Clearly the point of the parable, thus far, is the same as the point of the first two parables, God cares about the lost. In reality, however, this is a two-pronged parable, a parable that has two points. It seems as though this parable has a hook. It is one thing to understand that God cares about the lost. At this stage, the Pharisees and scribes in Jesus' audience could well be saying, "God cares about the lost, but we don't give a flip about them. They really don't matter to us; they are not our concern." With the final portion of the parable, Jesus has them all hooked.

It is at this point that Jesus gives us the other side of the story, the second half of the story.

LUKE 15:25-32

[25]"Now his older son was in the field, and when he came and approached the house, he heard music and dancing. [26]"And he summoned one of the servants and *began* inquiring what these things could be. [27]"And he said to him, 'Your brother has come, and your father has killed the fattened calf because he has received him back safe and sound.' [28]"But he became angry and was not willing to go in; and his father came out and *began* pleading with him. [29]"But he answered and said to his father, 'Look! For so many years I have been serving you and I have never neglected a command of yours; and *yet* you have never given me a young goat, so that I might celebrate with my friends; [30]but when this son of yours came, who has devoured your wealth with prostitutes, you killed the fattened calf for him.' [31]"And he said to him, 'Son, you have always been with me, and all that is mine is yours. [32]"But we had to celebrate and rejoice, for this brother of yours was dead and *has begun* to live, and *was* lost and has been found.'"

Notice the older brother has stayed at home. He has been faithful; he has worked all along. He hears the music and the dancing. Those at the feast are all dancing in a circle like *Fiddler on the Roof*. They are all excited; it is a wonderful time. The brother is reasoning, "What's going on here? A party? I wasn't invited to the party." The servants tell him, "It's your brother who's come back again. Your father's killed the fatted calf. He's received him back safe and sound." But the older brother is angry and he refuses to go in. His father comes out and pleads with him, "You need to come to this party we're having for your brother." The older son still refuses.

A missionary friend who works in Tanzania told me that he had recently decided to preach a series of sermons on the parables of Jesus in Luke. It was a new experience for him, and the results were surprising. When he had finished his sermon on this parable, he provided some time for questions and answers. One lady in the audience responded that the older brother had insulted his father as much as the younger brother had. Yes, the younger son had run away and wasted his father's possessions, but the older son had refused to do what his father asked. That was an insult to his father. My friend said it amazed him how frequently those in Africa got the point while Americans missed it. Their culture was so much more like the culture of Jesus' day.

The older son contends that his father is treating his younger brother in a way that makes him feel unappreciated, "Look, for so many years I've been serving you and I've never neglected one of your commands. Yet, you have never given me a goat so that I might celebrate with my friends. When this son of yours came who has devoured your wealth with prostitutes, you killed the fatted calf for him." One does not see much love on the part of the older brother either for his father or his brother. He fails to appreciate the joy of being with his father. It is a matter of "I've done what you told me to do so I'll get what I ought to get." His classic line is "Yet, you never have given me a goat so that I might celebrate with my friends but you gave this son of yours a fatted calf." Notice he addresses his brother not as "this brother of mine" but "this son of yours." A paraphrase in modern parlance might be: "You've never provided me with hot dogs and hamburgers for a party with my friends, and yet this guy comes back and you bring out the steaks. It's not fair; it's not right." The complaint continues: "He's devoured your wealth with prostitutes." Now, how does he know that? He assumes the worst of his brother. We do know from our text that he spent his money on "unsaved living," profligate living, but we are not told that he has wasted it on prostitutes. It is entirely possible that he did just that. The brother assumes the absolute worst of his brother.

The father's response is designed to help this older son rethink his situation. "Everything I have is yours." Your brother has wasted his inheritance and so now everything that is left belongs to you. What are you worried about? That is, of course, part of the older brother's concern. Indeed it is all his; why should his brother enjoy any of it?

The father continues, "We had to celebrate." Notice his desire to set things straight. He describes the younger son as "this brother of yours" not "this son of mine." He has turned the tables. Jesus makes it clear with this one statement the direction He intends for the parable. He has attempted to move His audience from "God cares about the lost" to the next step. "Your brother has begun to live. He was lost; he's been found." It is a wonderful occasion of celebration.

"God cares about the lost" and now "so should you." Notice how well that fits into the context of Luke 15. Our first question to ask as we study the parables of Jesus is "What was going on in the life of Jesus that produced this parable?" The answer is simple: They were complaining about Jesus eating with these tax collectors and sinners. Jesus gives these three parables to illustrate the fact that God cares about the lost. He puts a hook in the last parable that is designed to catch them. They have assumed parable one, parable two, and parable three will be just alike. But the third parable does not end as they would have guessed. Back comes the haunting message, "So should you." It is this author's assumption that these three are probably not collected and grouped here by Luke, but probably were told by Jesus on the same occasion. The first parable, the parable of the lost sheep, is told also on another occasion in Matthew. There the context is different. Likely Jesus simply had a good story and used it more than once.

Our second question is "What was going on in the life of the early church that would have led the evangelist to record this parable?" Again that is relatively easy. Luke was facing a church that still had a large Jewish population. Those Jewish Christians were having a hard time admitting Gentiles. He wants them to learn the lesson Jesus had taught to the Pharisees and scribes.

"What is the point of the parables?" God cares about the lost and so should believers, in Jesus' day. And "what is the message for us?" If God is reigning in our lives and in our churches, we will reach out to the lost, to those from the wrong side of the tracks.

One of the things that makes these parables so amazing is that Jesus tells parables that will touch tender hearts in both of His audiences. The tax collectors and sinners will see themselves in the lost sheep, the lost coin, and the younger brother. They will recognize that God loves them and is calling them home. Pharisees and scribes with tender hearts, yes there were some who had such hearts, would recognize that they, like the older brother, need to appreciate what they have. That is, in terms of relationship with the Father, to care about those who are out of relationship with Him, and to rejoice when they respond to the good news of God's love.

Parable of the Good Samaritan

In chapter 1 we began our study with a look at this parable as Origen, Augustine, Jerome and others allegorized it. Unfortunately their approach has caused many readers to miss Jesus' point. It is now time to try the methodology recommended in this book to arrive at Jesus' intended message.

In the 1960s, Clarence Jordan began an experiment. He was tired of all the turmoil of the civil rights movement of his day. He wanted to develop a community where Christians, black and white, could live together, work together, and worship together. He and a group of followers moved to Georgia to establish a farm where folks would live together much like in a commune, blacks and whites. He concluded that the majority of folks, when they read the Bible, did not understand it because language, environment, lifestyles, and geography were so foreign to them. Where are all of those places—Jerusalem, Bethlehem, Nazareth, and Capernaum? Who are Pharisees, Sadducees, Samaritans, Jews, Gentiles? Jordan decided to make a translation, really a paraphrase, of the New Testament that would speak to people of his day. His work was known as *The Cotton Patch Version*. He would transfer ancient places, things, and people to modern-day parallels. He made everything happen in, of all places, Georgia, and he made the problems between Samaritans and Jews, Gentiles and Jews, into black-white problems of his own era. Black and white problems would be easy for his audience to understand. His paraphrase is not the version one would choose for serious study of the Bible, but it does open the eyes of the reader to his own situation. One of the best sections of his work is his paraphrase of the parable of the Good Samaritan.[15] It provides a good way for us to begin our study of the parable. Be sure to read the clever footnotes Jordan provided.

> One day a teacher of an adult Bible class got up and tested him with this question: "Doctor what does one do to be saved?"
>
> Jesus replied, "What does the Bible say? How do you interpret it?"
>
> The teacher answered, "Love the Lord your God with all your heart and with all your soul and with all your physical strength and with all your mind; and love your neighbor as yourself."
>
> "That is correct," answered Jesus. "Make a habit of this and you'll be saved."
>
> But, the Sunday school teacher, trying to save face asked, "But . . . er . . . but . . . just who *is* my neighbor?"
>
> Then Jesus laid into him and said, "A man was going from Atlanta to Albany and some gangsters held him up. When they had robbed him of his wallet and brand-new suit, they beat him up and drove off in his car, leaving him unconscious on the shoulder of the highway.
>
> "Now it just so happened that a white preacher was going down the same highway. When he saw the fellow, he stepped on the gas and went scooting by."[16]
>
> "Shortly afterwards a white gospel song leader came down the road, and when he saw what happened, he too stepped on the gas.[17]
>
> "Then a black man traveling that way came upon the fellow, and what he saw moved him to tears. He stopped and bound up his wounds as best he could, drew some water from his water-jug to wipe away the blood and then laid him on the back seat.[18] He drove on into

---

[15] Clarence Jordan, *The Cotton Patch Version of Luke and Acts: Jesus' Doings and the Happenings* (New York: A Koinonia Publication, 1969), pp. 46-47.

[16] His homiletical mind probably made the following outline:
I don't know the man.
I don't wish to get involved in court proceedings.
I don't want to get blood on my new upholstery.
The man's lack of proper clothing would embarrass me upon my arrival in town.
And finally, a minister must never be late for worship services.

[17] What his thoughts were we'll never know, but as he whizzed past, he may have been whistling, "Brighten the corner, where you are."

Albany and took him to the hospital and said to the nurse, 'You all take care of this white man I found on the highway. Here's the only two dollars I got, but you all keep account of what he owes, and if he can't pay it, I'll settle up with you when I make a payday.'

"Now if you had been the man held up by the gangsters, which of these three—the white preacher, the white song leader, or the black man—would you consider to have been your neighbor?"

The teacher of the adult Bible class said, "Why, of course, the nig—I mean, er . . . well, er . . . the one who treated me kindly."

Jesus said, "Well, then, *you* get going and start living like that."

Jordan's *Cotton Patch Version* of this parable does help readers in the twenty-first century to feel something akin to what Jesus' audience might have felt on hearing Jesus tell the story.

LUKE 10:25-29

[25]**And a lawyer stood up and put Him to the test, saying, "Teacher, what shall I do to inherit eternal life?"** [26]**And He said to him, "What is written in the Law? How does it read to you?"** [27]**And he answered, "YOU SHALL LOVE THE LORD YOUR GOD WITH ALL YOUR HEART, AND WITH ALL YOUR SOUL, AND WITH ALL YOUR STRENGTH, AND WITH ALL YOUR MIND; AND YOUR NEIGHBOR AS YOURSELF."** [28]**And He said to him, "You have answered correctly; DO THIS AND YOU WILL LIVE."** [29]**But wishing to justify himself, he said to Jesus, "And who is my neighbor?"**

The word lawyer here is used for an expert in the law, not lawyer in the sense we would use the word today, i.e., a jurist, a person who goes to court. Instead the term is used of an expert in the Law—Genesis through Deuteronomy.

The lawyer stands up to test Jesus with a question, "Teacher, what shall I do to inherit eternal life?" The question was much debated by the rabbis. Jesus in turn asks the lawyer a question. Since the man was an expert in the Law, he should be able to determine the message for himself. The lawyer's answer is very much like the conclusion the rabbis had reached. "You shall love the Lord your God with all your heart, with all your soul, with all your strength and

---

[18] All the while his thoughts might have been along this line: "Somebody's robbed you; yeah, I know about that, I've been robbed, too. And they done beat you up bad; I know, I've been beat up, too. And everybody just go right on by, leaving you laying here hurting. Yeah, I know. They passed me by, too."

with all your mind and your neighbor as yourself." Jesus tells him that he has indeed read the Law correctly and concludes with "Do this and you will live."

The man, however, wishes to justify himself and his attack on Jesus. In an effort to put Jesus on the spot, he asks, "Who is my neighbor?" He, like many of the Jews in his day, wished to make the circle of neighbors very small. It would include only fellow Jews, and then only fellow Jews of the same persuasion, here likely only Pharisees. One can see something of this attitude in Jesus' teaching in the Sermon on the Mount. "You have heard that it was said, 'Love your neighbor and hate your enemy.' But I say to you, Love your enemies" (Matt. 5:43-44). This parable provides an interesting commentary on the words of Jesus there.

Notice it is this question that produces the parable. The question provides us with the answer to our question, "What was going on in the life of Jesus that produced the parable?" In reality Jesus will not quite answer the man's question. Instead He will answer the question the man should have asked.

LUKE 10:30-37

[30]Jesus replied and said, "A man was going down from Jerusalem to Jericho, and fell among robbers, and they stripped him and beat him, and went away leaving him half dead. [31]"And by chance a priest was going down on that road, and when he saw him, he passed by on the other side. [32]"Likewise a Levite also, when he came to the place and saw him, passed by on the other side. [33]"But a Samaritan, who was on a journey, came upon him; and when he saw him, he felt compassion, [34]and came to him and bandaged up his wounds, pouring oil and wine on *them*; and he put him on his own beast, and brought him to an inn and took care of him. [35]"On the next day he took out two denarii and gave them to the innkeeper and said, 'Take care of him; and whatever more you spend, when I return I will repay you.' [36]"Which of these three do you think proved to be a neighbor to the man who fell into the robbers' *hands*?" [37]And he said, "The one who showed mercy toward him." Then Jesus said to him, "Go and do the same."

Notice that the man in the parable is "going down" from Jerusalem to Jericho. One always goes down from Jerusalem, no matter which direction he is headed, and always up when going to Jerusalem. The elevation of Jerusalem is indeed up when compared to everything that surrounds it. Jews tended to view Jerusalem as the pinnacle of the universe. Jericho in biblical times was a kind of resort city. Since priests and Levites inherited no homeland, many chose to live in Jericho. The road from Jerusalem to Jericho is very winding. The distance "as the crow flies" is only about fourteen miles and by road about seventeen miles. It was common for thieves to hide behind the limestone rocks along the winding wilderness road. In Bible times, the road came to be called "the path [ascent] of blood," probably because it was considered unsafe.

The man in the parable has been robbed and left there half dead. Jesus provides little information about the man. Is he a Jew? Is he a Pharisee? Is he a priest? Is he a Roman? Those who will pass by cannot identify the man's family, tribe, nationality, or religious standing. After all, the man has even been stripped of his clothing.

By chance a priest was going on that road, perhaps heading from Jerusalem where he has served home to Jericho. When he saw the man, he passed by on the other side. The man had likely just been at worship, but that worship does not translate into action. He might well have justified his action by saying, "If I touch a dead body, I'll be unclean and I can't offer sacrifice. I can't function in my role as priest."

Likewise, a Levite also came to the place, saw the man, and passed by on the other side. Priests and Levites alike were from the tribe of Levi. Levites, however, did not function as priests. There had always been far too many men in the tribe of Levi for all of them to function as priests. The Levites often sang songs, performed temple responsibilities, and even managed temple budgets. They, like the priests, would have been deemed important religious leaders, men who were to be examples for the community. This man too passed by on the other side.

But a Samaritan who was on a journey came upon the man. The appearance of a Samaritan in the story is surprising. One might have expected the third character to be an Israelite since there is an often-repeated formula in Judaism: priest, Levite, Israelite.[19] The enmity between Jews and Samaritans in the first century AD was proverbial. The rabbis had proclaimed, "He that eats the bread of the Samaritan is like one who eats the flesh of swine."[20] There is a long history of this bitterness and resentment. When the Assyrians deported the leading citizens of Israel in 722 BC, those who remained intermarried with non-Jews. These people became religious syncretists, mixing the religion of the Canaanites with worship to Yahweh God. When Jews returned from Babylonian captivity during the rebuilding of the temple, the Samaritans opposed the Jews. By the time of Nehemiah the hatred of Samaritans was deep and strong. The Samaritans built their own place of worship on Mount

---

[19] Bernard Brandon Scott, *Hear Then the Parable: A Commentary on the Parables of Jesus* (Minneapolis: Fortress, 1989), p. 189.
[20] *M. Sheb.* 8.10 (Danby, 49).

Gerizim. During the intertestamental period, one of the Macabbean kings, John Hyrcanus, destroyed the Samaritan temple. Thus the bad blood continued to develop. Herod the Great added a Samaritan woman to his long list of wives, which may suggest the relationship between Jews and Samaritans had improved. During the reign of the procurator Coponius (AD 6-9), it again worsened when Samaritans disrupted temple worship by strewing human bones in the temple during the celebration of the Passover. In Jesus' day, Samaritans hated Jews, and Jews hated Samaritans.

The Samaritan was such an unwholesome person in Jewish eyes that one would never have expected him to stop and help this injured man. He felt compassion on the man. He bandaged up his wounds, pouring oil and wine on them. He put the man on his own beast, brought him to the inn, and took care of him. The oil was used as a kind of ointment, and the wine as a disinfectant. He brought him to the inn to take care of him. An inn in the first century was basically a place to tie up and feed one's animals on a journey. Again this man is not a fellow one would have expected to stop at all. The common Jewish attitude of the day was that Samaritans are all bad people.

On the next day, the Samaritan took out two denarii and gave it to the innkeeper. He said, "Take care of him. Whatever more you spend, when I return, I will repay you." Two denarii, again, was wages for two days' labor at minimum wage. The "two dollars" *The Cotton Patch Version* is misleading. In reality it would be more like offering $80.00, a good sum of money, for the man's care.

Jesus asked the man, "Which of these three do you think proved to be the neighbor to the man who had fallen among the robbers' hands?" The man responded, "The one who showed mercy to him." Notice that the man cannot even bring himself to say "the Samaritan." Jesus says, "Go do the same thing."

Notice the man's original question was "Who is my neighbor?" Jesus does not really answer that question. Instead He answers the question, "How should a neighbor behave?" The parable is really about who proved to be neighbor, an interesting twist to the story.

In Luke's day, Jewish Christians would have felt comfortable declaring fellow Jewish Christians their neighbors and their brothers. They would not have been so inclined regarding Gentile Christians.

Just who is my neighbor? Well, everyone is my neighbor. And how should I respond to my neighbor? I should respond in love and care.

LIVING IN GOD'S REIGN

1. How does reading all three "lost parables" in Luke 15 together change one's understanding of those parables?

2. It has been suggested that the portion of the parable of the prodigal son church members most need today is the part about the other brother. Do you believe that is so? If so, why?

3. Jesus told the three lost parables in such a way that everyone in His audience could get something meaningful for their lives—the Pharisees and scribes and the tax collectors and sinners. Discuss the skill with which Jesus told His parables.

4. Do you believe that Christians today, like the lawyer to whom Jesus gives the parable of the good Samaritan and the Jews in Jesus day, would like to make their circle of neighbors as small as possible? Discuss the significance of such a quest.

CHAPTER 8

When God Reigns . . . My Money and My Things

The American way of living is to compartmentalize everything. This is work; this is family; this is play; this is my religious life. God is not a category that touches every part of my life. A crucial question for the believer is "How does God's reign relate to all of the things in my life?" Jesus is determined to help His disciples see that every part of their lives is touched by the kingdom and placing it first in their lives.

Parable of the Rich Farmer

LUKE 12:13-15

   ¹³Someone in the crowd said to Him, "Teacher, tell my brother to divide the *family* inheritance with me." ¹⁴But He said to him, "Man, who appointed Me a judge or arbitrator over you?" ¹⁵Then He said to them, "Beware, and be on your guard against every form of greed; for not *even* when one has an abundance does his life consist of his possessions."

The reader cannot be sure exactly what the man was asking of Jesus. Was he asking Jesus to get his brother to divide the family inheritance 50-50, really going beyond the requirements of the law? Had the older brother taken all of the inheritance instead of just the double portion that was due him? Had the older brother, from the viewpoint of the younger, taken more than his share? Whatever the case, this man felt he had been treated unfairly and wanted Jesus to step in and set things right. He had come to Jesus to get things resolved.

Jesus asks the man a legitimate question, "Man, who appointed Me a judge or an arbiter over you?" You see, there are judges, arbitrators, whose job it was to solve those kinds of problems. Jesus is simply telling the man he can follow the legal avenues available to him. He is telling the man, "That is not My job."

It is at that point that Jesus offers a warning, not only to the man, but also to his whole audience: "Beware and be on guard against every form of greed." Greed is the hunger for more, wanting what is not rightly yours. Jesus has cut to the heart of the matter. The man's problem was greed, the all-consuming desire for more. Jesus goes on to tell His audience, "For not even when one has an abundance does his life consist of his possessions." That is a difficult lesson for Americans to learn. We are convinced a happy life consists of possessing things. The more we possess the happier we think we will be. This desire for possessions is really the heart of what is going on in our story. It sets the stage for the parable that follows. Real life is not measured by possessions.

LUKE 12:16-21

[16]**And He told them a parable, saying, "The land of a rich man was very productive. [17]"And he began reasoning to himself, saying, 'What shall I do, since I have no place to store my crops?' [18]"Then he said, 'This is what I will do: I will tear down my barns and build larger ones, and there I will store all my grain and my goods. [19]"And I will say to my soul, "Soul, you have many goods laid up for many years *to come*; take your ease, eat, drink *and* be merry." ' [20]But God said to him, 'You fool! This *very* night your soul is required of you; and *now* who will own what you have prepared?' [21]So is the man who stores up treasure for himself, and is not rich toward God."**

A real danger in interpretation of this parable rests in the assumption of many that the parable is designed to address rich people. We are very quick to point out to those around us that we are not rich, despite the fact that most of us are rich by standards used in most parts of the world. From the historical context, the parable is given by Jesus to address the man who comes to Jesus asking Him to divide the family wealth. This man is not rich. The other brother seems to have the wealth. The man in our parable is one who is without. The parable was designed to address not the "haves" but the "have-nots." Jesus is addressing the one who would say, "If I just had . . . , then I'd be happy." Jesus argues, "That doesn't make for happiness."

The parable begins with a rich man whose farm is very productive. Notice the emphasis in what the man says to himself: "What shall **I** do, since **I** have no place to store **my** crops? . . . This is what **I** will do, **I** will tear down **my** barns and build larger ones. There **I** will store **my** grains and **my** goods. **I** will say to **my** soul, 'Soul you have many goods laid up for many years to come. Take your ease, eat drink and be merry.'" His reasoning resounds with "I" and "my." Here is a man who has not thought beyond today and the possessions that he has. He assumes that, because he has possessions, he has everything that really matters. People do not matter. God has no place in his plans. He says, "I'm just going to store it all away, live off of it, and enjoy myself."

This is not a parable about preparing for one's retirement. That is not the point Jesus desires for His hearers to take home with them. There is nothing wrong with saving for one's retirement. There is nothing particularly wrong with tearing down a barn and building a larger barn. The difficulty is the man's attitude, his assumption that life is composed of what one possesses.

God said to the man, "You fool, this very night your soul is required of you. Now who will own what you have prepared? Who's going to get it? When you are gone, whose will it be? Your family may or may not appreciate it."

Jesus drives home the message of the parable and the lesson He wants to teach by concluding, "So is the man who stores up treasure for himself and is not rich toward God." In the context of Luke 12, Jesus is saying to the man who thought, if he could just get his inheritance, he would be happy, "Life is not made up of things." That is not what makes for real happiness.

It is at this point that Jesus preaches a little sermon to His disciples:

LUKE 12:22-34

²²And He said to His disciples, "For this reason I say to you, do not worry about *your* life, *as to* what you will eat; nor for your body, *as to* what you will put on. ²³"For life is more than food, and the body more than clothing. ²⁴"Consider the ravens, for they neither sow nor reap; they have no storeroom nor barn, and *yet* God feeds them; how much more valuable you are than the birds! ²⁵"And which of you by worrying can add a *single* hour to his life's span? ²⁶"If then you cannot do even a very little thing, why do you worry about other matters? ²⁷"Consider the lilies, how they grow: they neither toil nor spin; but I tell you, not even Solomon in all his glory clothed himself like one of these. ²⁸"But if God so clothes the grass in the field, which is *alive* today and tomorrow is thrown into the furnace, how much more *will He clothe* you? You men of little faith! ²⁹"And do not seek what you will eat and what you will drink, and do not keep worrying. ³⁰"For all these things the nations of the world eagerly seek; but your Father knows that you need these things. ³¹"But seek His kingdom, and these things will be added to you. ³²"Do not be

afraid, little flock, for your Father has chosen gladly to give you the kingdom. [33]"Sell your possessions and give to charity; make yourselves money belts which do not wear out, an unfailing treasure in heaven, where no thief comes near nor moth destroys. [34]"For where your treasure is, there your heart will be also."

As He has on numerous occasions, Jesus uses a "lesser than, greater than argument." If God takes care of those birds we would deem inconsequential, the ravens, surely He will take care of you. People are of more value than those birds.

"Which of you by worrying can add a single hour to his life span?" Literally, the text says which of you by worrying can "add a single cubit" to his life? Jesus could be saying, "Can you add a cubit, 18 inches, to your height by worrying?" If the distance had been smaller, this option would have been more likely. The other option is to see Jesus using a metaphor to describe one's life as a line with birth on one end and death on the other. He then asks, "Can you, by worrying, add 18 more inches to your life line?" Thus many modern translations demonstrate this understanding:

> ". . . can add a *single* hour to his life's span" NASB
> ". . . can add a single hour to his life" NIV
> ". . . add a single hour to your span of life?" NRSV

Jesus tells them, "If then you cannot accomplish such a very little thing, why do you worry about other matters? God will take care of you." Life is not made up of the things about which you worry.

Jesus again offers another "lesser than, greater than argument." Solomon with all of that wonderful clothing, all those royal colors, is not clothed like the beautiful wild flowers. If God so clothes the grass in the field with beautiful flowers, and that grass is alive today and tomorrow is thrown into the furnace, how much more will He clothe the believer? Surely He cares more about the believer than the grass that grows wild on the hill. The historical context brings light to the text here. In the first century AD, especially in Palestine, one did not have a lot of wood to waste. One simply did not chop down wood to burn in his fire. One would collect the dry grass, tie it up, and toss it in to burn. In Palestine the grass grows and is very green during the rainy season, November through about January. There are the later rains in March and April, but beyond that, when June rolls around, there is no green grass. It is all dried up. It is good for nothing except burning.

Jesus calls for His followers not to be consumed in seeking the necessities of life. The Gentiles or pagans (literally "nations") spend their time seeking such things, and rightly so because they do not have a sense of a God who knows their needs, loves them, and will care for them. Instead Jesus' followers are to seek God's kingdom, that is His reign in their lives, and all these things God will provide.

The man in the parable obviously was not seeking God's reign. He thought life was made up of possessions. He had missed what was really important.

Jesus refers to believers as His "little flock" and tells them that their heavenly Father has chosen gladly to give them His reign. Because of that they are to sell their possessions and give to charity and in so doing to make for themselves money belts that will not wear out. They will then have an unfailing treasure in heaven where no thief can steal and no moth can destroy. It is at that point in the little sermon that Jesus gives a wonderful summary of His lesson and of the point of the parable: "For where your treasure is, there will your heart be also." The word "heart" is used in Jewish and Greek literature in a different way than we would use it today in English. We use the heart to talk about one's feelings. On Valentine's Day, people send Valentine cards that have a heart on them because we think of the heart as the place of emotions and feelings. For the Jews of Jesus' day, the heart was where one makes his decision. The mind was where one thought; one decided with his or her heart and felt with his or her belly. Older English translations of the Bible frequently refer to "bowels of compassion," a very literal translation of the original Hebrew or Greek. That is where one feels and experiences the emotion of fondness. Our text, however, uses the word "heart." It might be paraphrased "Where your treasure is, there will your decisions be made also." In reality that is very logical. It would be a bit redundant to say, "For where your treasure is there will your feelings be or there is located what you like." Jesus is telling His disciples that their decisions are based on what they most value. And so it is today—we decide based on our priorities.

Parable of the Unjust Steward

LUKE 16:1-9

¹Now He was also saying to the disciples, "There was a rich man who had a manager, and this *manager* was reported to him as squandering his possessions. ²"And he called him and said to him, 'What is this I hear about you? Give an accounting of your management, for you can no longer be manager.' ³"The manager said to himself, 'What shall I do, since my master is taking the management away from me? I am not strong enough to dig; I am ashamed to beg. ⁴"I know what I shall do, so that when I am removed from the management people will welcome me into

their homes.' ⁵"And he summoned each one of his master's debtors, and he *began* saying to the first, 'How much do you owe my master?' ⁶"And he said, 'A hundred measures of oil.' And he said to him, 'Take your bill, and sit down quickly and write fifty.' ⁷"Then he said to another, 'And how much do you owe?' And he said, 'A hundred measures of wheat.' He said to him, 'Take your bill, and write eighty.' ⁸"And his master praised the unrighteous manager because he had acted shrewdly; for the sons of this age are more shrewd in relation to their own kind than the sons of light. ⁹"And I say to you, make friends for yourselves by means of the wealth of unrighteousness, so that when it fails, they will receive you into the eternal dwellings."

The parable begins with the phrase "Now He was also saying to the disciples . . ." Jesus is again talking with the twelve. The larger context is His teaching regarding wealth. How should one value riches and how should he handle them? Apparently, Luke was also concerned about how his audience, the Christians who would read this Gospel, would handle riches. Luke has more to say about riches than any of the other Gospel writers.

The rich man in our story has a manager or a steward whose job it was to handle his financial affairs. A steward is someone put in charge of managing someone else's goods. Our English word steward has a most interesting etymology. It comes from two English words "sty" and "ward," and would have originally referred to one who takes care of someone's pigs. The rich man had received a report that his manager was squandering his possessions. So he calls in the manager and tells him, "What is this I hear about you? Hand over the books. I want an audit of everything. You are out of a job."

The manager begins to talk to himself and reason what he should do, "What shall I do? My master is taking away my job as manager. I'm not strong enough to dig. I have had this nice job way too long to do that. I just don't have the strength. And begging is just below my dignity. I mean, I've worked for a rich man and circulated with all the upper crust. I know what I'll do, so that when I lose my job, people will come to me and still welcome me into their homes. I will make friends." So the manager summons those who owe his master for goods he has provided. He asks the first debtor, "How much do you owe my master?" The man tells him, "One hundred measures of oil." The manager tells him, "Take your bill and sit down quickly and write fifty." He asks a second debtor, "How much do you owe?" The man says, "One hundred measures of wheat." The manager tells this man, "Take your bill and write eighty." When he learns of what the manager has done, his master praised the unrighteous manager because he had acted shrewdly.

Many readers of this parable are troubled by the fact that the master praises "an unrighteous manager." They are also troubled that Jesus would use a wicked man as an example of a desired character trait for believers. This has led them to misunderstand the nature of the parable. Some have attempted to rehabilitate the manager and claim that his actions are noble. Since Jews were not to charge their fellow Jews interest, some have suggested that the manager has simply removed the interest that his master had charged. Notice that Jesus, in the parable, says that the master praised the "unrighteous manager."

On the surface it seems that one debtor got a better deal than the other. The first debtor's bill was marked down 50%, while the other's bill was only marked down 20%. This is troublesome to some readers. Many have noted that 50 measures[21] of oil and 20 measures[22] of wheat would have been valued at approximately the same amount. In reality, even if one debtor did get a better deal than other, this does not affect the interpretation of the parable.

The man in the parable is clearly an unrighteous manager, but even this unrighteous man has planned ahead to make things work out for his good. The key word in the text is "shrewd" or "prudent." It is the same word used by Jesus in the parable of the wise man who built his house on the rock and of the wise virgins who brought the extra oil as they awaited the return of the bridegroom. On all of these occasions, the word is translated "wise." And in each parable, someone has prepared for the future.

Jesus goes on, "For the sons of this age are more shrewd in their relations to their own kind than the sons of light." The folks of the world who are wicked sometimes act more shrewdly or prudently. They know what they want and plan to get it. Unfortunately "the sons of light," believers, fail to exercise the same concern and plan to accomplish the noble tasks before them.

Jesus goes on to say to His disciples, " . . . make friends for yourselves by means of the wealth of unrighteousness," literally "mammon of unrighteousness" or "unrighteous mammon." In so doing when the wealth fails, they will be received "into the eternal dwellings." I once heard a teacher use this text to argue that one should take advantage of ill-gotten gains so that he could make friends and would then in turn have friends in hell. Such an interpretation clearly misses the point.

The phrase "unrighteous mammon" or "wealth of unrighteousness" can be confusing to the modern reader. The word "mammon" means money. It

---

[21] The Greek word for "measure" here is *batos* (βάτος). Each "measure" would be approximately 8 gallons.

[22] This time the Greek word for "measure" is *koros* (κόρος). Each "measure" would be 10-12 bushels.

is simply a Hebrew word spelled out with Greek characters and then ultimately English characters. It is coupled with the adjective "unrighteous" in the Dead Sea Scrolls to talk about money because the pursuit of money often leads to unrighteousness. Many gain it unrighteously and use it unrighteously.

Believers need to use this money to make friends for themselves up in heaven. Jesus had earlier taught the same lesson: "So it is with those who store up treasures for themselves but are not rich toward God" (Luke 12:21).

The manager in the parable is not praised for his dishonesty but for his shrewdness. It is the fact that he knew how to take advantage of the circumstances and to plan for the future. Christians, as believers, often use their possessions in ways that indicate that they are not preparing for the future that is supposed to be so important to them. They have missed what really matters.

LUKE 16:10-13

> [10]"He who is faithful in a very little thing is faithful also in much; and he who is unrighteous in a very little thing is unrighteous also in much. [11]"Therefore if you have not been faithful in the *use of* unrighteous wealth, who will entrust the true *riches* to you? [12]"And if you have not been faithful in *the use of* that which is another's, who will give you that which is your own? [13]"No servant can serve two masters; for either he will hate the one and love the other, or else he will be devoted to one and despise the other. You cannot serve God and wealth."

Jesus continues His explanation: "He who is faithful in a very little thing is faithful also in much." It is interesting that Jesus would term money as a "very little thing." We tend to see it as something very big and very important. If someone does not take care of money, he should not be expected to take care of what really matters. "Therefore, if you have not been faithful in the use of unrighteous wealth, who will entrust true riches to you?" True riches are something other than physical riches. After all, our possessions are not really our own; they are God's. Just as the manager in our story was using someone else's wealth, so we are using another's wealth.

Believers must learn that no servant can serve two masters. Jesus tells them that the servant will either hate the one master and love the other or else he will be devoted to one and despise the other. One cannot serve God and wealth.

Notice the contrast that is so common in Hebrew. Because the Hebrew language does not have comparative adjectives and has no good way of making comparisons, in Hebrew one uses dire contrast to make a point—here the dire contrast between hate and love. One must love one more than the other.

One cannot have two masters on an equal level. When the two masters give opposing orders, there will come a time when one must decide which master he will obey. One cannot serve God and wealth, mammon, at the same time.

In the next paragraph, we will learn that Pharisees who were lovers of money were listening to all these things. They scoffed at Jesus, saying, "Oh, Jesus you just don't understand. It's just because you don't have money that you're talking the way you talk. Wealth is important." While one can take advantage of wealth for good, these people had missed this vital lesson.

Parable of the Rich Man and Lazarus

Luke 16 continues with yet another parable concerning riches, the parable of the rich man and Lazarus. The first parable in this chapter, the unrighteous manager, was followed by comments on the parable and a lesson on possessions. This parable, by contrast, is preceded by comments that introduce the parable. The audience is no longer the disciples, but the Pharisees who are scoffing at Jesus. The Pharisees would undoubtedly see their wealth as a mark that God was blessing them. Their possessions validated their claim of faith. Jesus and the Pharisees differed on their theological interpretation of wealth and possessions.

LUKE 16:14-18

¹⁴Now the Pharisees, who were lovers of money, were listening to all these things and were scoffing at Him. ¹⁵And He said to them, "You are those who justify yourselves in the sight of men, but God knows your hearts; for that which is highly esteemed among men is detestable in the sight of God. ¹⁶"The Law and the Prophets *were proclaimed* until John; since that time the gospel of the kingdom of God has been preached, and everyone is forcing his way into it. ¹⁷"But it is easier for heaven and earth to pass away than for one stroke of a letter of the Law to fail. ¹⁸"Everyone who divorces his wife and marries another commits adultery, and he who marries one who is divorced from a husband commits adultery."

Jesus responds to the scoffers by telling them that they are trying to make themselves look good in the eyes of those who see them as religious leaders, but God knows their hearts. God's priorities and human priorities are not the same. What people praise is not what God will praise. Here we see great reversal that is so much a part of Luke—those on the top are really on the bottom; those on the bottom will be on the top. What people value is not what is really to be valued. The Pharisees found in Deuteronomy what they believed was a gospel of wealth—they had concluded that the righteous prosper and the wicked suffer.[23]

Jesus goes on to tell them that the law and the prophets were proclaimed until John. It was Jesus' contention that they were misreading the Old Testament. He blessed the poor and taught that believers should share what they have with those in need. Since the time of John, the good news of the kingdom of God had been preached. Jesus said that everyone was "forcing his way into it," a phrase that Craddock has suggested might be paraphrased as the "multitudes are storming the door."[24] Although there is a debate as to whether the text indicates everyone is trying to force his or her way into God's reign or everyone is doing violence, Craddock's suggestion seems best to fit the context. Jesus is not arguing that He is giving a teaching that supersedes the law. Indeed, "it is easier for heaven and earth to pass away than for one stroke[25] of the letter of the law to fail." His difference with the Pharisees is over correct interpretation of the law.

The move to a discussion of divorce and remarriage seems a bit abrupt in a discussion of possessions and wealth unless one recognizes the difficulty Jesus has with the Pharisees. Their interpretation of the law can easily be seen in their interpretation of texts about divorce. Jesus is arguing, "You folks misunderstand the nature of the law. You're trying to push your way and your wishes, but you're not taking seriously what God says." Jesus uses adultery as an illustration of their misreading of the law. The one who divorces his wife and marries another commits adultery. Adultery is a word for marital unfaithfulness. "He who marries the one who is divorced from a husband commits adultery." Again, the language seems very harsh to us. Many today would like to soften Jesus' words. There is not much of a way to make His words more palatable for a society where divorce is so prevalent. He is telling the Pharisees, "You read the law in such a way to make divorce easy. That is not God's intent. He does not want divorce among His people. You will be judged by the very Scriptures you are using as you seek to justify yourselves." This theme will return at the end of the parable. Jesus will now try to teach the Pharisees something of His understanding of wealth.

The situation that leads to Jesus' giving the parable is people who are scoffing at Him because they have money and they think that possessions are what really matter.

---

[23] See Deuteronomy 13:1-5.

[24] Fred B. Craddock, *Luke*, Interpretation: A Bible Commentary for Teaching and Preaching (Louisville: John Knox Press, 1990).

[25] A part of a letter that distinguishes it from another—e.g., in English the difference between an "O" and a "Q."

LUKE 16:19-26

[19]"Now there was a rich man, and he habitually dressed in purple and fine linen, joyously living in splendor every day. [20]"And a poor man named Lazarus was laid at his gate, covered with sores, [21]"and longing to be fed with the *crumbs* which were falling from the rich man's table; besides, even the dogs were coming and licking his sores. [22]"Now the poor man died and was carried away by the angels to Abraham's bosom; and the rich man also died and was buried. [23]"In Hades he lifted up his eyes, being in torment, and saw Abraham far away and Lazarus in his bosom. [24]"And he cried out and said, 'Father Abraham, have mercy on me, and send Lazarus so that he may dip the tip of his finger in water and cool off my tongue, for I am in agony in this flame.' [25]"But Abraham said, 'Child, remember that during your life you received your good things, and likewise Lazarus bad things; but now he is being comforted here, and you are in agony. [26]"And besides all this, between us and you there is a great chasm fixed, so that those who wish to come over from here to you will not be able, and *that* none may cross over from there to us.'"

The parable begins like the last one with a rich man. This rich man feasts everyday, not just special days. He wears purple all the time. Purple and fine linen normally were worn only by rich people and even then only on special occasions. He is a rich man who has everything.

The second character is a poor man named Lazarus. The man is obviously a beggar whose malady makes it necessary for others to bring him and lay him at the gate of the rich man. His body is covered with sores.

We have been referring to this story of the rich man and Lazarus as a parable. This is the only parable of Jesus in the New Testament where a proper name is mentioned—in fact, two proper names, Lazarus and Abraham.

There are those who argue that this is not a parable; Jesus is speaking from a real-life experience. They argue that this parable does not begin as the parables of Jesus normally do. It starts "Now there was a rich man . . ." They also argue that a man is named is this parable, something Jesus does not normally do. Therefore, this is not a parable.

These objections are quite easily countered. This parable begins as Luke typically begins a parable. For example, in Luke 12:16 a parable begins "Now the land of a certain rich man," and in Luke 16:1 another parable begins "There was a rich man who had a manager . . ."

The fact that the poor man's name is given here probably indicates something of the great reversal that is so common in Luke. We do not even know the rich man's name, but we know the name of the poor man, Lazarus. He is someone who really matters. Despite the fact that the Latin Vulgate describes the rich man as "Dives," Latin for "rich man," his name is never given. The name Lazarus really stands for Eleazar, which means literally "God is my help." The poor man may simply have been given a name to indicate his importance.

Lazarus is a poor man. He was laid at the rich man's gate every day because rich people would come to visit the rich man, and hopefully they would have pity on this poor man and give him some benevolence. Lazarus' body was covered with sores. He longed to be fed from the crumbs that might be falling from the rich man's table. Those crumbs may have been a little bigger than one might think. In the first century AD, men would use bread to mop up the gravy and juices. The bread also served as a napkin to wipe their hands. What was left was thrown to the ground for the dogs to eat. Lazarus longs for anything that might fall from the table. His situation was so bad that even the dogs would lick his sores. Dogs in the first century AD were not pets. Dogs were pests, a roving mob. One of the worst names a Jew could think to call someone was "dog." In fact, a typical epitaph for Gentiles was "You dogs!" Lazarus does not have the strength to even shoo the dogs away.

Jesus gives a dramatic description of Lazarus' death: "Now the poor man died and was carried away by the angels to Abraham's bosom." Notice that here again we see a reversal. The parable began with a description of the rich man, then we learn of the poor man, Lazarus. But in describing their deaths, Jesus begins with the state of the poor man, and only then does He move on to the rich man. The structure forms an A-B-B-A, a literary devise used for emphasis called a chiasm. The poor man makes a grand exit from this life. He is carried by angels, and he ends up in Abraham's bosom. Next comes the death of the rich man. Notice again the reversal. One would expect a marvelous funeral for the rich man. The rich man dies, and we are simply told that he is buried. Notice the contrast—poor man dies, is carried away by angels, and is taken to Abraham's bosom; the rich man dies and is buried.

The rich man finds himself in Hades (the realm of the dead, a term equivalent to the Old Testament Hebrew word "Sheol"). He lifted up his eyes, being in torment, and he saw Abraham from afar and Lazarus in his bosom. That is not what he would have expected. After all, he was the blessed man, and he was sure that meant he was righteous. Jewish literature typically painted a picture of heaven and hell in such a way that heaven and hell were in sight of one another. Such an arrangement made heaven all the grander and hell all the worse.

The situation of the rich man is something he has never before endured. He cries out and says, "Father Abraham have mercy on me. Send Lazarus so that he may dip the tip of his finger in water and cool off my tongue for I am in agony in this flame." The rich man still sees Lazarus as his boy who will come and do his bidding. Lazarus is no better than a slave to fulfill his desires. His attitude has not changed a lot. The situation of the rich man is a very bad one.

Abraham calls the rich man to remember the life he had lived and the kind of life Lazarus had been forced to live. In the first century AD some Jews believed that once a year Abraham would go to the other side and bring Jews (notice there was no second chance for Gentiles) who repented in hell back to the other side. He had extra merits, brownie points, that could cover their sins—a situation a little like those today who want to depend upon the merits of the saints. In this parable, that simply is not the case. One's fate is fixed by the kind of life he lived. Abraham indicates this by saying, "Besides all this, between us and you there is fixed a great chasm so that those who wish to come over from here to you are not able and none may cross over from there to us." There is no chance of changing one's state; there is no second chance.

It is unfortunate that many would like to take this parable as the explanation of exactly what happens when one dies. They argue at death there are two temporary states, paradise (or Abraham's bosom) and torment, basing this claim upon this parable and the statement of Jesus to the repentant thief as he hung from a cross, "Today you will be with Me in paradise." They then argue that, when the judgment day rolls around, everyone receives a body and comes to the judgment seat. Those in paradise, this temporary waiting place, will be called up to heaven, and those in torment will ultimately be sent to hell. The difficulty with this theory is that Jesus' audience would not have understood this parable in that way. For His audience paradise, Abraham's bosom, was equal to heaven, and torment was equal to hell. What happens to me when I die? Well, there really is not a clear indication from anywhere in the Bible. There are passages in Paul where he says "To die is to be with Christ" and yet there are other passages that say that, when Jesus returns, all of those who are dead in Christ will first be caught up, will first be raised, and then those who are alive will meet them up in the heavens.

There is no simple solution to the problem. The problem may be complicated by the fact that, when I die, I move from a realm of time to a realm where there is no time. The explanations of what happens at death in Scripture are given to time-bound creatures. It is imperative that we not try to make something out of the parable that Jesus would never have intended. I may never know the exact configuration of what will happen to me when I die. But as a believer, I can say, "I'll be with Jesus, and that's good enough for me."

This parable is one of the parables I like to call "two-pronged parables," like the parable of the prodigal son that we have already studied. The first point is clear. The way one uses his wealth, his possession, will affect his eternal destiny. One needs to be shrewd as the last parable taught. But the parable continues.

LUKE 16:27-31

[27]"And he said, 'Then I beg you, father, that you send him to my father's house—[28]for I have five brothers—in order that he may warn them, so that they will not also come to this place of torment.' [29]"But Abraham said, 'They have Moses and the Prophets; let them hear them.' [30]"But he said, 'No, father Abraham, but if someone goes to them from the dead, they will repent!' [31]"But he said to him, 'If they do not listen to Moses and the Prophets, they will not be persuaded even if someone rises from the dead.'"

Since the rich man's first request could not be granted, he responded with another, "Then I beg you father that you send him to my father's house for I have five brothers, in order that he may warn them so that they will not also come to this place of torment." The rich man still sees Lazarus as his servant. He may not have had concern about poor folks like Lazarus, but he does care for his own family. He does not want them to end up like he has. Abraham tells him, "They have Moses and the prophets, let them hear them." They have the law, just as do the Pharisees Jesus is addressing. The very law they use to justify themselves will judge them. It provides them with all they need in terms of living the faithful life. The rich man, knowing his brothers and their approach to the law, said to Abraham, "No, father Abraham but if someone goes to them from the dead, they will repent." But Abraham replies, "If they do not listen to Moses and the prophets they will not be persuaded even if someone rises from the dead."

The two prongs of this parable are evident. The first is the simple message that the way you live your life and the way you handle the possessions God has given you will determine your eternal state. Once this life is over there is no changing that. God will rectify things. All things will be set right. There will be a grand reversal on the other side. But the second point focuses on Abraham's statement that even if someone is raised from the dead, some folks will not believe. Many of those standing there before Jesus will not be convinced when Jesus is raised from the dead. Their hearts are wrong. Here Jesus is giving His audience a taste of what will happen with His own death which is now just around the corner. Even when He comes back from the dead, there will be folks who will not become believers—no matter what one does, no matter what one says.

It is interesting that, just weeks after Jesus told this parable, another Lazarus will be raised from the dead (John 11). Instead of that event causing the religious leaders of the day to become believers, they seek to kill Him. He had become a walking signpost inviting others to believe in Jesus.

In our own day, many see their wealth as what is really important. Jesus says that is just not the case. It is one's relationship with God that matters. There will be a grand reversal for many of those who are rich in terms of this world but are spiritually poor, and for many of those who are poor in this world but have stored up treasures in heaven.

LIVING IN GOD'S REIGN

1. Discuss the standard most Americans use for measuring "true happiness."
2. Contrast the importance of planning for the future while at the same time striving not to be like the rich farmer.
3. How can the Christian move beyond worrying about the necessities of life?
4. Discuss the meaning of "where your treasure is there your heart will be also." How does what matters most to me affect my decisions?
5. How should the believer use and view his wealth in terms of preparing for the future?
6. Discuss why one character in the parable of the rich man and Lazarus is given a name while the other is not. Discuss the great reversal that is so much a part of Luke's Gospel.

CHAPTER 9

When God Reigns . . . My Talents and My Opportunities

Not only did Jesus want His disciples to see that the kingdom informed their understanding of their money and their possessions, He wanted them to learn God's reign in their lives would affect their exercise of their talents and their opportunities.

The next two parables (Matt. 25:14-30; Luke 19:12-26) are related parables although they fall in different historical situations. Despite many similarities, there are some significant differences. There are those who argue that Luke simply adapted the parable in Matthew; that seems most unlikely because the parables seem to have slightly different points.

Parable of the Talents

The first parable that we will examine is the parable of the talents. A talent is a weight that, when used of silver or gold, came to mean an amount of money. A talent was equal to 6,000 denarii. It is interesting to consider the etymology of our English word "talent." An English dictionary will indicate that the word "talent" comes from a Hebrew word *talenta*, which came to English via Greek. It originally referred to a weight of silver or gold. In English "talent" has come to mean "one's ability." It is the parable of Jesus that has given our English word its meaning. Again one can see how the parables of Jesus have affected the English language.

MATTHEW 25:13

"**Be on the alert then, for you do not know the day nor the hour.**"

The setting for this parable is a larger section in which Jesus is teaching His disciples the need for being ready for His return. Immediately after the parable of the virgins waiting for the return of the bridegroom (Matt. 25:1-13), Jesus tells them, "Be on alert then for you do not know the day or the hour for it is just like a man about to go on a journey." He is arguing that the second coming will be at a time that believers cannot know. The parable of the talents is designed to call believers to be ready.

MATTHEW 25:14-30

[14]"For it is just like a man *about* to go on a journey, who called his own slaves and entrusted his possessions to them. [15]"To one he gave five talents, to another, two, and to another, one, each according to his own ability; and he went on his journey. [16]"Immediately the one who had received the five talents went and traded with them, and gained five more talents. [17]"In the same manner the one who *had received* the two *talents* gained two more. [18]"But he who received the one *talent* went away, and dug *a hole* in the ground and hid his master's money.

[19]"Now after a long time the master of those slaves came and settled accounts with them. [20]"The one who had received the five talents came up and brought five more talents, saying, 'Master, you entrusted five talents to me. See, I have gained five more talents.' [21]"His master said to him, 'Well done, good and faithful slave. You were faithful with a few things, I will put you in charge of many things; enter into the joy of your master.'

[22]"Also the one who *had received* the two talents came up and said, 'Master, you entrusted two talents to me. See, I have gained two more talents.' [23]"His master said to him, 'Well done, good and faithful slave. You were faithful with a few things, I will put you in charge of many things; enter into the joy of your master.'

[24]"And the one also who had received the one talent came up and said, 'Master, I knew you to be a hard man, reaping where you did not sow and gathering where you scattered no *seed*. [25]'And I was afraid, and went away and hid your talent in the ground. See, you have what is yours.'

[26]"But his master answered and said to him, 'You wicked, lazy slave, you knew that I reap where I did not sow and gather where I scattered no *seed*. [27]'Then you ought to have put my money in the bank, and on my arrival I would have received my *money* back with interest. [28]'Therefore take away the talent from him, and

give it to the one who has the ten talents.'

²⁹"For to everyone who has, *more* shall be given, and he will have an abundance; but from the one who does not have, even what he does have shall be taken away. ³⁰"Throw out the worthless slave into the outer darkness; in that place there will be weeping and gnashing of teeth."

The master called his slaves and entrusted them with his possessions. He gave one slave five talents, another two and another one, "each one according to his ability." Notice Jesus' use of the word "ability." One can easily see how our modern English word "talent" came to mean "ability." The master then immediately went off on a journey. The man who had received five talents went and traded with them, and he gained five more. If a talent is equal to 6,000 denarii, this man would have $1,260,000²⁶ to invest, a huge sum. He invested that money and doubled it. In the same way, the second servant received the two talents, $504,000. He invested that money and gained two more talents. The man who received one talent, $252,000, dug a hole in the ground and hid his master's money. He, by the way, was following an adage from the rabbis, "the only safe depository for money was a hole in the ground."

Now after a long time, the master returned to settle accounts with his slaves. The one who had received five talents brought the five talents he had been given plus the five he had earned. His master said to him, "Well done, good and faithful slave, you were faithful in a few things, I will put you in charge of many. Enter into the joy of your master." It is interesting that the master would term $1,260,000 "a few things." Again this follows the pattern elsewhere in the New Testament that would see money as lesser riches or lesser blessings. Similarly the one who had received two talents came up to his master and said, "Master you entrusted two talents to me; I have gained two more." The master responds, "Well done, good and faithful slave. You were faithful in a few things, I will put you in charge of many things; enter into the joy of your master." Finally the one who received the one talent came to his master and said, "Master, I knew that you are a hard man, reaping where you don't sow and gathering where you scattered no seed. I was afraid. I went and hid your talent in the ground. See here is your money." The master answered and said to him, "You wicked, lazy slave" [by the way in Greek, wicked and lazy rhyme]. "You have said yourself that I reap where I did not sow and gather where I did not scatter seed. You knew that, and yet you did not invest my

---

²⁶ 5 talents X 6,000 denarii/talent X $42.00 (assuming minimum wage at $5.25/hour and 8 hours of work per day).

money. At least you could have put it in the bank [literally "at the tables," probably the location where money was exchanged] to earn interest." The master instructed his servants, "Therefore take away the talent from him and give it to the one who has ten talents."

It may well seem a little unfair to us to give this man's talent to the one who has more. "For everyone who has, more shall be given and he will have an abundance but from the one does not have, even what he has will be taken away. Throw out the worthless slave into outer darkness. There will be weeping and gnashing of teeth." From the context, one ought to use his talents, his abilities, and so be prepared for the second coming, the return of the Lord. Each slave is given according to his ability. One uses what he was given and he gains; another uses and he gains. The parable teaches that the issue is not how many talents or how much ability one has. The believer is called to exercise some risk and use what he has been given. The believer cannot simply play it safe. It is the using that matters.

Parable of the Minas

This parable has some similarities with the parable of the talents but also some significant differences. It falls on the heels of the story of Zaccheus, a rich tax collector. Zaccheus has a sense of what matters that causes him to be willing to give away his wealth and to follow Jesus.

LUKE 19:11
> [11]**While they were listening to these things, Jesus went on to tell a parable, because He was near Jerusalem, and they supposed that the kingdom of God was going to appear immediately.**

This parable also has implications for one's understanding of the second coming. Those who were listening to Jesus had a misunderstanding of the nature of the kingdom of God. They were looking for an eschatological end and an earthly reign that would be immediate. They had no room for the spiritual transformation Jesus was teaching, which would reach its culmination only in His return.

LUKE 19:12-26
> [12]**So He said, "A nobleman went to a distant country to receive a kingdom for himself, and *then* return. **[13]**"And he called ten of his slaves, and gave them ten minas and said to them, 'Do business *with this* until I come *back.*' **[14]**"But his citizens hated him and sent a delegation after him, saying, 'We do not want this man**

to reign over us.' [15]"When he returned, after receiving the kingdom, he ordered that these slaves, to whom he had given the money, be called to him so that he might know what business they had done. [16]"The first appeared, saying, 'Master, your mina has made ten minas more.' [17]"And he said to him, 'Well done, good slave, because you have been faithful in a very little thing, you are to be in authority over ten cities.' [18]"The second came, saying, 'Your mina, master, has made five minas.' [19]"And he said to him also, 'And you are to be over five cities.' [20]"Another came, saying, 'Master, here is your mina, which I kept put away in a handkerchief; [21]for I was afraid of you, because you are an exacting man; you take up what you did not lay down and reap what you did not sow.' [22]"He said to him, 'By your own words I will judge you, you worthless slave. Did you know that I am an exacting man, taking up what I did not lay down and reaping what I did not sow? [23]'Then why did you not put my money in the bank, and having come, I would have collected it with interest?' [24]"Then he said to the bystanders, 'Take the mina away from him and give it to the one who has the ten minas.' [25]"And they said to him, 'Master, he has ten minas *already*.' [26]"I tell you that to everyone who has, more shall be given, but from the one who does not have, even what he does have shall be taken away.'"

The historical situation in the first century AD makes this story come to life. One could not become a king without receiving permission from Rome. In fact, one of Herod the Great's sons, Archelaus, had hoped to take the title king and to rule over Judea, the southern region of his father's kingdom. When his father died, the kingdom had been divided among Herod's sons. The Jews of Judea objected to having Archelaus as king. They sent emissaries to Rome, saying, "We don't want him to be king." Archelaus came back to Judea, not as king, but with the title *ethnarc*, a lesser title equal to something like "ruler of a people." Jesus may well be playing off of the Archelaus story with which His audience would have been familiar.

This time the prospective king called together ten of his slaves. He distributed ten minas among them, with each receiving one mina. A mina appears in some older English translations as "a pound." It is valued at approximately one hundred denarii. The NIV notes its value as "three months' wages." Using our system of valuation, it would be approximately $4,200. Each slave is given the same amount, one mina. This time there is no mention of each receiving money according to his ability. The master instructs them,

"Do business with this until I come back."

At this point in the parable, Jesus turns to the prospective king's citizens. They hated him, and they sent a delegation after him (to Rome we would assume) saying, "We do not want this man to reign over us." When he returned, after receiving his kingdom, the master ordered that the ten slaves to whom he had given the money be called to him so that he might know what business they had done. It is interesting that the parable records the results of only three of the ten slaves. These three characters are sufficient to make Jesus' point. The first appeared saying, "Master your mina has earned ten minas more." Now that is quite a profit, taking one mina, $4,200 and making ten minas, $42,000. The master said to him, "Well done, good slave, because you have been faithful in a very little thing you will have authority over ten cities." He will now be the local ruler over ten city-states. The second slave came to the master saying, "Your mina has earned five minas." Again the profit is amazing—from $4,200 he has earned an additional $21,000. The master told him, "You will be over five cities." There are those who have suggested that this slave is not praised as much because he was not as faithful. That is not the point of Luke recording this parable. This man also has taken advantage of the opportunity given to him. A third slave came to the master saying, "Master, here is your mina which I kept and put away in a handkerchief." Notice the details that Luke preserves. The slave put the money in a handkerchief and hid it away. He then gives his reason for such behavior, "For I was afraid of you because you are an exacting man. You take up where you do not lay down and reap what you don't sow." The language here sounds very much like the one-talent man in the parable of the talents. Like the master in the parable of the talents, the master in this parable responds, "By your own words I will judge you, you worthless slave. Did you know that I am an exacting man, taking up where I do not lay down and reaping what I don't sow? Then why did you not put my money in the bank [literally, at table] so that, when I returned, I could have collected it with interest." The master said to the bystanders, "Take the mina away from him and give it to the one who has ten minas." Again their response is like ours might have been, "Master, he already has ten."

Jesus concludes this portion of the parable with these words of instruction, "I tell you whoever has more will be given, and from the one who does not have, even what he has will be taken away." Jesus then finishes the story by returning to those who did not want the master to be king.

LUKE 19:27

[27]"But these enemies of mine, who did not want me to reign over them, bring them here and slay them in my presence."

Notice that this parable is another two-pronged parable. First the message to those who are his slaves who are called to use what has been given to them. The second is to those who refuse to let the king reign over them. Those who have refused the new king will be slain in his presence. Jesus, it would seem, has two audiences in mind: those who would claim to be His subjects and those who refuse His rule. The parable began with the ten slaves, turned to the citizens, back to three of the ten slaves and then finished with the citizens.

In the parable of the talents, we discovered Jesus' concern for the exercise of one's ability. If there is a difference, the minas may well represent opportunities because everyone gets the same amount. In the parable of the talents, the concern was not in how much the person made, but in the use of the money, the talent. Those who are praised have responded according to their ability. The message is "Take advantage of what you have. Use what God has given you." Again, in a context very much like the parable of the talents, Jesus gives the parable of the minas. The context produces a slightly different parable. One parable does not seem to be simply an adaptation of the other. The message here seems to be a call for believers to be prepared for His return by taking care of the opportunities that are bestowed upon them and a warning to those who refuse to accept Jesus as the Messiah King.

LIVING IN GOD'S REIGN

1. Discuss how the parables of Jesus have affected the English language. Which parables are so significant in our culture that they have changed the meaning or significance of words or phrases?
2. How do we express our faith in the way we use our talents?
3. It has been suggested that the parable of the talents demands that we take a gamble in using our talents. Respond to this suggestion.
4. In addition to our talents, God is concerned with the use of the opportunities that come our way. Discuss the similarities and differences that comprise the use of our talents and the use of our opportunities.

CHAPTER 10
When God Reigns, His People Will Pray

When God reigns in believers' lives, His people will pray. This chapter will examine three very brief parables concerning prayer. All three parables appear in Luke. It is significant that Luke places a special emphasis on prayer in the life of Jesus and the early church in Luke and Acts.

Parable of the Friend at Midnight

The context for the first parable in this chapter is a question which Jesus' disciples ask.

LUKE 11:1-4

¹It happened that while Jesus was praying in a certain place, after He had finished, one of His disciples said to Him, "Lord, teach us to pray just as John also taught his disciples." ²And He said to them, "When you pray, say:
'Father, hallowed be Your name.
Your kingdom come.
³Give us each day our daily bread.
⁴And forgive us our sins,
For we ourselves also forgive everyone who is
indebted to us.
And lead us not into temptation.'"

Jesus has just finished praying. Prayer is so much a part of His life that one of the disciples asks, "Lord, teach us to pray just as John taught his disciples to pray." Jesus provides a model prayer. The concern of the prayer is not so much what to pray but how to pray—what are the elements of good prayers, what are the concerns?

The prayer here differs slightly from the one Jesus gives in the Sermon on the Mount (Matt. 6:9-13). In fact it looks as though Luke may have abbreviated this version of the prayer. It seems as though Luke may simply have left out the second line of synonymous parallelism, the manner by which Jews would make a poem. The Lord's Prayer is very much a poem; many modern translations format it as one. Luke seems to have left out the repeating lines. For example, the line "your kingdom come" is followed in Matthew by "your will be done." In reality, those two sentences express the same thought. Luke leaves out the second line. Later in the prayer, Jesus says according to Matthew, "lead us not into temptation" followed by "but deliver us from evil." Luke omits the second line that simply furthers the thought of the first line.

Jesus provides His disciples with a poem prayer that can easily be remembered. You will notice the request for personal things is very simple. "Give us today enough bread for today." "Forgive us our sins." The heart of the prayer is that God's name will be honored and hallowed, deemed holy, and that His kingdom, His reign, will come.

LUKE 11:5-13

⁵Then He said to them, "Suppose one of you has a friend, and goes to him at midnight and says to him, 'Friend, lend me three loaves; ⁶for a friend of mine has come to me from a journey, and I have nothing to set before him'; ⁷and from inside he answers and says, 'Do not bother me; the door has already been shut and my children and I are in bed; I cannot get up and give you *anything.*' ⁸"I tell you, even though he will not get up and give him *anything* because he is his friend, yet because of his persistence he will get up and give him as much as he needs. ⁹"So I say to you, ask, and it will be given to you; seek, and you will find; knock, and it will be opened to you. ¹⁰"For everyone who asks, receives; and he who seeks, finds; and to him who knocks, it will be opened. ¹¹"Now suppose one of you fathers is asked by his son for a fish; he will not give him a snake instead of a fish, will he? ¹²"Or *if* he is asked for an egg, he will not give him a scorpion, will he? ¹³"If you then, being evil, know how to give good gifts to your children, how much more will *your* heavenly Father give the Holy Spirit to those who ask Him?"

Luke begins this parable in a way very typical for his Gospel, "Suppose one of you has . . ." Several of his parables begin, "Suppose a certain man . . ." He does not follow the pattern so common in Matthew, "the kingdom of heaven is like. . . ."

Someone has gone on a journey and comes to a friend's home at midnight. This would not have been at all unusual in the first century AD. Before the days of air conditioners, to travel during the night because of the heat was normal. When he arrives at his friend's home, the friend immediately prepares to show good hospitality and to provide his visitor with some food. His cupboard is bare and so he sets out to another friend's home to ask for help, "My friend has come in here at midnight and I need some bread. I want three loaves for him." Perhaps you can remember visiting your grandmother or a great aunt who simply must set food before a guest. Such was the custom in the Ancient Near East. Three loaves of bread may sound like an enormous amount of bread to the modern reader. That may be a bit deceptive to us because, when we think of loaves of bread, we imagine the kind one would buy today at a grocery store. In biblical times a loaf of bread would have been more like a large muffin, and three loaves would have been deemed a normal meal for an adult male. In large communities made up of several extended families, one lady in the community would take her turn to bake bread so that the community would have fresh bread every day.

The man tells his neighbor-friend, "This friend of mine has come to me on a journey. I have nothing to set before him." Such a break in hospitality would be an insult from the friend and ultimately for the whole community.

From inside his house, the neighbor says, "Do not bother me; the door has already been shut [perhaps better translated 'locked'], and my children and I are in bed." Jesus demonstrates that He understood how poor folks lived. A typical house for common folks in the first century AD was about twelve-feet square. The whole family lived in the same room. It was their living room, their bedroom, their kitchen, their dining room. "We're all in bed" likely expressed reality. Apparently the neighbor had climbed over sleeping children and was talking through the window. "I cannot get up and give you anything. I would wake up the children. It is a terrible inconvenience."

Without sharing the neighbor's ultimate response, Jesus concludes by telling His audience how the man is bound to respond. "I tell you even though he will not get up and give him anything because he is his friend, yet because of his persistence, he will get up and give him as much as he needs." Being a friend is not enough to get him to go to all the bother, but he will respond to get rid of his bothersome neighbor. The danger here is to misread the parable and to assume that Jesus is telling His disciples that, if they bother God enough with prayers, He will finally give in to their requests. What might come to mind is the child in the supermarket who keeps pestering mom for some toy or breakfast cereal until the mother finally gives in and buys it for him. That would, however, miss the very nature of the parable. A very common way to make a point among Jews was to use a "lesser than, greater than" argument. The argument would go as follows, "if the lesser will do . . ., surely the greater will do that and more." Here, if an unwilling friend will grant a wish simply because of persistence, what will a loving God do for those who persistently pray to Him?

Jesus continues His explanation by telling His hearers ". . . ask and it will be given to you, seek and you will find, knock and it will be opened. For everyone who asks receives and he who seeks finds and to him who knocks it will be opened."

He continues with another illustration: "Suppose one of you fathers is asked by his son for a fish. He will not give him a snake instead of a fish, will he?" And the implied answer is "Of course not!" Fathers do not treat their sons that way. "If he's asked for an egg, he won't give him a scorpion will he?" Why, of course not! Fathers do not treat sons that way. "If you then being evil know how to give good gifts to your children, how much more will your heavenly Father give the Holy Spirit to those who ask." Notice this time the "lesser than, greater than argument" is explicit. Earthly fathers, even though they are sinners and make mistakes, give their children what they need. Surely your Father will give you what you need. He will give you His Holy Spirit to dwell in you and to transform you.

The message for the parable is simple: If the friend, who does not want to help you, will give in because you are persistent, surely a God who loves you and cares for you will answer your prayers if you are persistent. Jesus is concerned that the disciples will, as days go by, give up praying. He wants them to continue to pray diligently.

Parable of the Unrighteous Judge

The next parable is really a sister parable to the parable of the friend at midnight. This time the two parables fall into different contexts. This parable is usually called the parable of the wicked or unrighteous judge.

LUKE 18:1-8
    ¹**Now He was telling them a parable to show that at all times they ought to pray and not to lose heart, ²saying, "In a certain city there was a judge who did not fear God and did not respect man. ³"There was a widow in that city, and she kept coming to him, saying, 'Give me legal protection from my opponent.' ⁴"For a while he was unwilling; but afterward he said to himself, 'Even**

though I do not fear God nor respect man, ⁵yet because this widow bothers me, I will give her legal protection, otherwise by continually coming she will wear me out.'" ⁶And the Lord said, "Hear what the unrighteous judge said; ⁷now, will not God bring about justice for His elect who cry to Him day and night, and will He delay long over them? ⁸"I tell you that He will bring about justice for them quickly. However, when the Son of Man comes, will He find faith on the earth?"

Jesus gives this parable because He is concerned that the disciples will face discouragement and persecution. This may lead them to lose heart and stop praying. The parable is designed to teach the disciples, "Don't lose heart."

Widows in biblical times had few rights. The unscrupulous would often take advantage of them. The widow in this parable is seeking legal protection from the city judge.

This parable provides the reader with another "lesser than, greater than argument." The judge in the parable is clearly a bad man. He is not righteous, he does not care about people, and he does not care about God and His will. He gives in to the widow because she continues to ask.

The judge admits to himself that he is a wicked man, "I do not fear God nor respect man." It is the woman's persistence that wears him down (literally "she gives me a black eye"). We, however, have a God who is so unlike this judge. He cares for us, and He loves us. Surely if the lesser (the judge) answers a request, the greater (God) will do even more. God will surely bring about justice for His elect who cry to Him day and night. He will not delay long over them; He will bring about justice quickly. Now for the believer, the rescue never seems quick enough. The answer to prayer is not always as soon as we wish it were, but He does answer.

It is interesting that Jesus finishes the discourse with a dismal conclusion. "When the Son of Man comes will He find faith on the earth?" Will there still be folks praying? Will everyone have just given up? In the current historical situation, Jesus is concerned about His disciples. When He does not return as soon as they think He will, will they give up praying and lose heart?

The message is especially appropriate for Luke's church. If one moves to the situation of the early church 30 or even 40 years down the line and, despite their expectations, the Lord has not returned as soon as many have assumed, the real danger is that they, too, will stop praying and lose heart. The message is simple. Keep on praying. God cares. God will bring about justice; it will ultimately come "to those of us who cry to Him day and night."

Parable of the Pharisee and the Tax Collector

The third parable in this chapter falls on the heels of the second one. It is one of the best-known parables in all of the New Testament. The basic context is the teaching Jesus has just given regarding prayer. Luke provides his readers with a little more insight into the situation.

LUKE 18:9
   ⁹And He also told this parable to some people who trusted in themselves that they were righteous, and viewed others with contempt: . . .

In His audience, Jesus has some people who are convinced of their own righteousness and viewed others with contempt. They were basically patting themselves on the back. "Look what good people we are. Look at all that we have done. We deserve God's praise." They also look down at others; they turn up their noses, proclaiming these others as unworthy of God's blessings. Jesus gives them this parable to teach them an important lesson.

LUKE 18:10-14
   ¹⁰"Two men went up into the temple to pray, one a Pharisee and the other a tax collector. ¹¹"The Pharisee stood and was praying this to himself: 'God, I thank You that I am not like other people: swindlers, unjust, adulterers, or even like this tax collector. ¹²I fast twice a week; I pay tithes of all that I get.' ¹³"But the tax collector, standing some distance away, was even unwilling to lift up his eyes to heaven, but was beating his breast, saying, 'God, be merciful to me, the sinner!' ¹⁴"I tell you, this man went to his house justified rather than the other; for everyone who exalts himself will be humbled, but he who humbles himself will be exalted."

Three times each day, anyone who could would go to the temple to pray. In the parable, two drastically different men had come to the temple to pray—a Pharisee, a separatist who called for strict adherence to both the law and to the oral tradition that provided interpretation of the law; and a tax collector, an employee of the Roman government, a part of a profession that was deemed dishonest and as traitors to the Jewish nation.

The Pharisee stood and was "praying this to himself." Translations differ on whether the phrase should be translated "for himself," "to himself," or "about himself." The choice makes little difference in understanding the man and the nature of his prayer. He was clearly praying for his own benefit. "God, I thank you that I am not like other people: swindlers, unjust, adulterers or even like this tax collector. I fast twice a week; I pay tithes of all that I get." Probably the Pharisee was not any of those bad things he outlined. He was not a swindler. He was not unjust. He was not an adulterer. And above all, he was not a tax collector. He looks at himself and pats himself on the back and says, "Look what a good man I am."

He proclaims, "I fast twice a week." Although the law commanded a fast only on one day each year, the Day of Atonement, this man followed the normal practice of Pharisees in his day. In the first century AD, Pharisees would fast every Monday and every Thursday. It is interesting that the author of the *Didache*, an early Christian document written about AD 100 to 110, seems to have misunderstood the nature of Jesus' warning not to fast like the Pharisees (that is, fast for the show). He admonishes his readers not to fast like the Pharisees on Monday and Thursday, but instead to fast on Wednesday and Friday.

The Pharisee also says, "I pay tithes of all that I get." Again, one is reminded of the words of Jesus in Luke 11:42, "But woe to you Pharisees! For you pay tithe of mint and rue and every *kind of* garden herb, and *yet* disregard justice and the love of God; but these are the things you should have done without neglecting the others." The law demanded a tithe of all the major crops—grapes, olives, and wheat. It made no mention of the garden herbs, many of which came up "volunteer" each year. This man extended his tithe even beyond what was required of him.

Most of all though, the Pharisee says, "I thank you that I'm not like this tax collector." It is important to know that in the first century AD, people prayed out loud. In fact, even in the Old Testament, when Hannah was praying for a son, she prayed silently causing Eli to assume that she was drunk (1 Sam. 1:9-18). Since the Pharisee was praying out loud, the tax collector standing around the corner would have heard him praying this prayer. What a blow to one's ego!

The second man in the parable was a tax collector. Tax collectors in the first century AD were particularly hated. They were in alliance with the Roman government. Most believed that these scalawags were always taking advantage of them. There were no simple forms that one filled out to determine how much one owed in taxes. In fact, tax collecting was farmed out. One would bid on how much money he would collect for a certain region. He would then hire others, who worked under him. If extra money was collected, it would simply go into the pocket of the tax collector. These men could not be trusted. They were deemed dishonest and disloyal. They were generally held in disdain. Their connection with the Gentiles, the Romans, made them clearly unclean.

The tax collector is standing at some distance. He did not walk to the front. He felt so unworthy that he was even unwilling to lift up his eyes to heaven. The typical way to pray in the first century AD was to raise one's hands to heaven with palms up, indicating one brought nothing to God, and to look to heaven. Although there are a few passages in the Bible where someone prays with his head bowed, bowing one's head is a relatively recent phenomenon. Here is a man who does not raise his head. He beats his breast and says, "God be merciful to me a sinner." Notice he recognizes his own lost state. He realizes that he, on his own, has no value and no right to stand before a holy God.

Jesus' response drives home the point of the parable, "I tell you this man went to his house justified rather than the other, for everyone who exalts himself will be humbled and he who humbles himself will be exalted." Again, in the context, people were saying, "We are just because we are such good folks. We are righteous. We look down at these other bad people."

It is easy to recognize the place a parable like this would have had in the preaching of Paul, Luke's travel companion. The parable illustrates that the one who is indeed just is one who recognizes his own sin, who recognizes that he must turn to God for His grace, and that without that grace he would indeed be lost. The one who stands justified before God is the one who humbles himself. He will be exalted. The one who exalts himself will be brought low.

LIVING IN GOD'S REIGN

1. Discuss the difference between "pestering God" and "being persistent in prayer."
2. How does the view we hold of God and His willingness to answer our prayers affect the way we pray?
3. How does the Pharisee in the parable of the Pharisee and the tax collector illustrate that good deeds and a holy life are not enough?
4. What do you learn of grace from the parable of the Pharisee and the tax collector?

CHAPTER 11

What it Means to be a Disciple of the Kingdom

Jesus frequently uses parables to clarify the nature of discipleship. Despite the fact that masses of people followed Jesus from place to place and listened to His wonderful teachings, many had no sense of the life He was calling them to live. This chapter will examine several short parables that broach this subject.

Parable of the Wise and Foolish Builders

Jesus ends the Sermon on the Mount in Matthew 7 with a parable. That parable is designed to call followers to understand that professing allegiance to Jesus is not enough. An obedient lifestyle and a change of life are required.

MATTHEW 7:21-23

²¹**"Not everyone who says to Me, 'Lord, Lord,' will enter the kingdom of heaven, but he who does the will of My Father who is in heaven *will enter.* ²²"Many will say to Me on that day, 'Lord, Lord, did we not prophesy in Your name, and in Your name cast out demons, and in Your name perform many miracles?' ²³"And then I will declare to them, 'I never knew you; DEPART FROM ME, YOU WHO PRACTICE LAWLESSNESS.'"**

A lot of people are going to claim to be Jesus' disciples. They will not, however, prove to be His disciples unless they do what God says. Many will say, "We did wonderful things in your name, accomplished wonderful, miraculous tasks." Jesus will respond, "That's not enough. You have missed the point about what it means to be My disciples. I never knew you, depart from Me. Your lifestyle is what matters. You practice lawlessness." He then goes on to tell a brief parable.

MATTHEW 7:24-27

[24]"Therefore everyone who hears these words of Mine and acts on them, may be compared to a wise man who built his house on the rock. [25]"And the rain fell, and the floods came, and the winds blew and slammed against that house; and *yet* it did not fall, for it had been founded on the rock. [26]"Everyone who hears these words of Mine and does not act on them, will be like a foolish man who built his house on the sand. [27]"The rain fell, and the floods came, and the winds blew and slammed against that house; and it fell—and great was its fall."

The wise man in this parable chose to build his house on a rock, probably a more difficult building location than the other character chose in the story, perhaps up on a rocky plateau. When the rainy season arrived and the winds blew, his house stood secure because it was built on a secure foundation. The foolish man, however, takes some short cuts in constructing his house. He chose to build in a wadi. A wadi is a dry riverbed. During most of the year this location would be dry, flat, easily accessible, and clear of any obstacles to building. During the rainy season, November through January in Palestine, the wadi would become a raging river. This man built his house there. The rains came and the wadi quickly filled with water. Since the house sat on sand with no real foundation, when the water rose and the winds blew, the house fell. Jesus adds, ". . . and great was its fall."

The account in Luke differs at some significant points.

LUKE 6:46-49

[46]"Why do you call Me, 'Lord, Lord,' and do not do what I say? [47]"Everyone who comes to Me and hears My words and acts on them, I will show you whom he is like: [48]he is like a man building a house, who dug deep and laid a foundation on the rock; and when a flood occurred, the torrent burst against that house and could not shake it, because it had been well built. [49]"But the one who has heard and has not acted *accordingly*, is like a man who built a house on the ground without any foundation; and the torrent burst against it and immediately it collapsed, and the ruin of that house was great."

Both the authors tell the story in a way that will help their respective audiences to understand Jesus' point. In Matthew, probably following the words of Jesus more precisely because his audience would have used the same building techniques as Jesus', the two men choose as their building surface a rock plateau and a sandy dry river bottom. In Luke, the wise man dug deep and laid his foundation on rock. The foolish man built his house on the ground without any foundation. Luke's context demonstrates how houses might be built in Asia Minor, the land of his audience. He has not altered the meaning of the parable or how his audience should apply it. He simply made a minor adjustment to make the parable fit their understanding of house-building.

One who does not live a life of obedience may think he is taking the easy way out. But such a life will not stand when it is hit by the storms of life. The foundation required for discipleship is an obedient lifestyle.

Parables of the Tower and of the King Going to War

The next two parables are again sister parables, the parable of the tower and the parable of the warring king. They are told together, have the same basic lesson, and are designed to drive home that message.

LUKE 14:25-27

[25]**Now large crowds were going along with Him; and He turned and said to them,** [26]**"If anyone comes to Me, and does not hate his own father and mother and wife and children and brothers and sisters, yes, and even his own life, he cannot be My disciple.** [27]**"Whoever does not carry his own cross and come after Me cannot be My disciple."**

The situation in Jesus' life that will ultimately lead to the two parables is a mass of people following Him. Many of these people undoubtedly desire to see His miracles and hear His wonderful stories. Jesus was concerned that their commitment went no deeper. His response was, "If anyone comes to me and does not hate his own father and mother and wife and children and brothers and sisters, yes even his own life, he cannot be My disciple. Whoever does not carry his cross and come after me cannot be my disciple." The language of Jesus here in Luke seems quite harsh. Jesus has said that His disciples must "hate" their own family members. As noted already, part of the difficulty here rests in the fact that Hebrew does not have comparative adjectives and adverbs. There simply is not a good way to say "love less." The normal procedure is to make dire contrasts, e.g., God loved Jacob and hated Esau (Mal. 1:3; Rom. 9:13). In a parallel text in Matthew 10:35-38, Matthew paraphrases the words of Jesus to make this clear:

³⁵"For I came TO SET A MAN AGAINST HIS FATHER, AND A DAUGHTER AGAINST HER MOTHER, AND A DAUGHTER-IN-LAW AGAINST HER MOTHER-IN-LAW; ³⁶and A MAN'S ENEMIES WILL BE THE MEMBERS OF HIS HOUSEHOLD. ³⁷"He who loves father or mother more than Me is not worthy of Me; and he who loves son or daughter more than Me is not worthy of Me. ³⁸"And he who does not take his cross and follow after Me is not worthy of Me."

Jesus was not here suggesting that one must tear down family relationships. His point was that His disciples must put Him above family relationships. Disciples must put Him ahead of father and mother and wife and children and brothers and sisters. The two parables that follow are designed to help Jesus' audience to see the serious nature of such a commitment.

LUKE 14:28-30

²⁸"For which one of you, when he wants to build a tower, does not first sit down and calculate the cost to see if he has enough to complete it? ²⁹Otherwise, when he has laid a foundation and is not able to finish, all who observe it begin to ridicule him, ³⁰saying, 'This man began to build and was not able to finish.'"

No one would begin the task of building a wonderful tower without first thinking about the cost. This tower may have been used to store farming implements and to provide a lookout to protect a field or livestock, or it may have been a tower built on the wall of a city to guard against invaders.

Some may remember those who have begun to build a house but abandoned the process. I can remember a family near my parents' home years ago who dug the basement but never built the house. They had either not thought through the cost of what they were planning or had hit against some dire financial situation. Jesus told His audience that they needed to think through what it would mean to follow Him. If they were going to be His disciples, they would have to be willing to pay the cost. They must be willing to bear the hardships in terms of family, be willing to deal with friends denying them, be willing to take up their cross and follow Jesus.

Jesus provides a second parable to drive home the message:

LUKE 14:31-33

³¹"Or what king, when he sets out to meet another king in battle, will not first sit down and consider whether he is strong enough with ten thousand *men* to encounter the one coming

against him with twenty thousand? ³²"Or else, while the other is still far away, he sends a delegation and asks for terms of peace. ³³"So then, none of you can be My disciple who does not give up all his own possessions."

The sister parable continues the call to count the cost. A king going to war must determine how he can win. When that king is outnumbered two to one—twenty thousand to ten thousand, he must either determine a way to win by ambushing his opponent or decide to cut his losses and surrender. One must think ahead.

Jesus was again telling His audience that they must count the cost. They must be willing to give up their stuff, their possessions, if they are to be His disciples.

Parable of the Two Sons

The next parable also emphasizes the importance of obedience for the disciple.

MATTHEW 21:23-27

²³When He entered the temple, the chief priests and the elders of the people came to Him while He was teaching, and said, "By what authority are You doing these things, and who gave You this authority?" ²⁴Jesus said to them, "I will also ask you one thing, which if you tell Me, I will also tell you by what authority I do these things. ²⁵"The baptism of John was from what *source*, from heaven or from men?" And they *began* reasoning among themselves, saying, "If we say, 'From heaven,' He will say to us, 'Then why did you not believe him?' ²⁶"But if we say, 'From men,' we fear the people; for they all regard John as a prophet." ²⁷And answering Jesus, they said, "We do not know." He also said to them, "Neither will I tell you by what authority I do these things."

The historical context for this parable is the question that the religious leaders ask Jesus, "By what authority are you doing these things and who gave you this authority?" They want to know who gave Him the right—the right to cleanse the temple (Matt. 21:12-13), to perform the healings (Matt. 21:14), to allow children to say these things about Him (Matt. 21:15-16), to teach what He was teaching (Matt. 21:23). Jesus responds by telling them He will answer their question if they will answer one He poses to them, "What is the source of the baptism of John, from heaven or from men?" They recognize very quickly that Jesus has put them on the spot. If they would say John's baptism is from men, the people, who regard John as a prophet and who have already gone out to be baptized by him, would be up in arms. If, on the other hand, they were to say that John's baptism was from God, then Jesus would surely ask them, "Why didn't you believe in him?" They decide to run a roundabout by answering, "We don't know." Immediately Jesus has placed them in a bad situation with the people. Here are the religious leaders of the day, and they cannot tell us whether a teacher is a false prophet. Jesus responds, "Then I won't tell you by what authority I do these things." If they cannot make this decision about John and his claims, how can they possibly understand the authority Jesus is exercising?

These people who would have claimed to be God's people were not really hearing the wonderful Messenger of God, God's Son. They claimed to be His children, but were not doing His will.

MATTHEW 21:28-32

²⁸"But what do you think? A man had two sons, and he came to the first and said, 'Son, go work today in the vineyard.' ²⁹"And he answered, 'I will not'; but afterward he regretted it and went. ³⁰"The man came to the second and said the same thing; and he answered, 'I *will*, sir'; but he did not go. ³¹"Which of the two did the will of his father?" They said, "The first." Jesus said to them, "Truly I say to you that the tax collectors and prostitutes will get into the kingdom of God before you. ³²"For John came to you in the way of righteousness and you did not believe him; but the tax collectors and prostitutes did believe him; and you, seeing *this*, did not even feel remorse afterward so as to believe him."

Notice the connection between the question the religious leaders have asked and the parable. One son begins as a rebel. He simply says "No!" to his father. Later he comes to his senses, regrets his rebellion, and does what his father had asked. The second son responds to his father's request by saying, "I will do it, sir," but he never does what his father asked. Jesus asks these religious leaders which of the sons did his father's bidding. The answer was simple, "Why, of course, the first."

Hopefully these people will see themselves in the parable. They had not responded favorably to John, the messenger of God. They claimed to be good sons of God, but they did not obey. Others, however, had obeyed. They had gone out to John, heard his message, and repented. These folks were frequently the sinners and tax collectors—those who were like the first son, first saying "No" but then repenting. Saying that you will do God's will is not enough. Being a good son demands obedience as well.

Parable of the Landowner and the Tenants

In Matthew, on the heels of the parable of the two sons, comes the parable of the landowner and the tenants. Although the parable of the two sons does not occur in Mark and Luke, all three Gospels connect the parable of the landowner and the tenants to the question the religious leaders ask regarding Jesus' authority for doing what He did (Matt. 21:33-46; Mark 12:1-12; Luke 20:9-19). These leaders have clearly rejected Jesus and His message of the kingdom. It is that rejection which is at the heart of this parable.

MATTHEW 21:33-46

[33]"Listen to another parable. There was a landowner who PLANTED A VINEYARD AND PUT A WALL AROUND IT AND DUG A WINE PRESS IN IT, AND BUILT A TOWER, and rented it out to vine-growers and went on a journey. [34]"When the harvest time approached, he sent his slaves to the vine-growers to receive his produce. [35]"The vine-growers took his slaves and beat one, and killed another, and stoned a third. [36]"Again he sent another group of slaves larger than the first; and they did the same thing to them. [37]"But afterward he sent his son to them, saying, 'They will respect my son.' [38]"But when the vine-growers saw the son, they said among themselves, 'This is the heir; come, let us kill him and seize his inheritance.' [39]"They took him, and threw him out of the vineyard and killed him. [40]"Therefore when the owner of the vineyard comes, what will he do to those vine-growers?" [41]They said to Him, "He will bring those wretches to a wretched end, and will rent out the vineyard to other vine-growers who will pay him the proceeds at the *proper* seasons." [42]Jesus said to them, "Did you never read in the Scriptures,

'THE STONE WHICH THE BUILDERS REJECTED,
THIS BECAME THE CHIEF CORNER *stone*;
THIS CAME ABOUT FROM THE LORD,
AND IT IS MARVELOUS IN OUR EYES'?

[43]"Therefore I say to you, the kingdom of God will be taken away from you and given to a people, producing the fruit of it. [44]"And he who falls on this stone will be broken to pieces; but on whomever it falls, it will scatter him like dust." [45]When the chief priests and the Pharisees heard His parables, they understood

that He was speaking about them. ⁴⁶When they sought to seize
Him, they feared the people, because they considered Him to be
a prophet.

Verses 33-34 clearly allude to Isaiah 5:1-7 and Psalm 80:6-16, where
Israel is portrayed as God's vineyard. Jesus' parable is simply an adaptation of
an old theme. The landowner takes real care to protect his vineyard. He builds
a wall to keep out animals, constructs a watchtower to guard against thieves
and fire, and digs a wine press to squeeze the grapes right on the spot. He is
convinced that his vineyard will bear fruit. The tenant farmers are to take care
of the vineyard while the owner is absent. They will pay rent in kind by giving
the landowner his share of the produce.

The landowner sends his slaves "to collect his fruit." Mark even specifies
"some of the fruit of the vineyard," that is, his share. Mark's account differs a
little from Matthew's. He mentions one servant sent at a time but says that
many others were also sent. In Matthew, Jesus says that the tenants beat one
slave, killed another, and stoned a third. One easily sees the killing of the
prophets which is well attested in the Old Testament (1 Kgs. 18:4, 13; Jer.
26:20-23; 2 Chr. 24:21-22). The landowner sends more slaves, an even larger contingency. "Last of all" (NIV) he sends his son. He feels the tenants will
surely respect him. Just as the rejection of the son by the tenants is the final
straw that brings the wrath of the landowner, so the rejection of the Son by
the religious leaders brings divine wrath on them.

For perhaps six months Jesus has been telling His disciples that the rulers
at Jerusalem would kill Him (Matt. 16:21; 17:23; 20:18). Now He tells the
rulers themselves, via this parable. At some level, the leaders understand Jesus'
message (vv. 45-46).

Jesus asks, "Have you never read?" and quotes from Psalm 118:22-23. At
this point Luke adds a paraphrase of Isaiah 8:14. Jesus turns to the image of a
building. The "capstone" (literally, "head of the corner") is most probably the
keystone at the top of an arch. Such a strangely shaped stone, which might
make a perfect fit in this specialized spot, would be kicked around as useless
by the builders. Psalm 118 may originally have been written about David—
rejected as king or warrior by many builders: Samuel, David's own family, Saul,
and Goliath. Though he was overlooked and rejected, he was chosen by God.
Another option involves seeing Israel as the rejected stone—despised by the
surrounding nations, but chosen by God. In the same way that David and/or
Israel were rejected, the builders in Jesus' day (leaders of the Jewish people)
rejected Him.

Matthew alone provides further explanation found in verse **43**. The religious leaders had failed so badly in handling God's "vineyard" and rejecting His Son that God would give the responsibility to another people who would produce the fruit of the kingdom.

Jesus' words are confirmed by the fact that "the chief priests and the Pharisees"—the two principal groups from which the religious leaders came in Jesus' day—understood this parable was about them. The Capstone would fall on them and grind them to dust.

Instead of heeding Jesus' warning, the leaders seek ways to arrest Him, although they are prevented because of their fear of the people who accept Jesus as a prophet.

Parables of the Patched Garment and the Old Wine in New Wineskins

The next two parables occur in all three of the Synoptic Gospels—in Matthew, Mark and Luke. We live in an era in which change lurks around every corner. It is amazing to see how differently people respond to change. Some are resistant, others hesitant, while yet others welcome it. The gospel Jesus preached presented His audience with a significant change from the religion they had heard preached by most rabbis of their day.

Luke's version of these two parables differs most from the other two, and he provides a concluding aphorism that does not appear in the other two. We will examine Luke's version of the parables and note the differences in Matthew and Mark.

LUKE 5:30-35

[30]The Pharisees and their scribes *began* grumbling at His disciples, saying, "Why do you eat and drink with the tax collectors and sinners?" [31]And Jesus answered and said to them, "*It is* not those who are well who need a physician, but those who are sick. [32]"I have not come to call the righteous but sinners to repentance."

[33]And they said to Him, "The disciples of John often fast and offer prayers, the *disciples* of the Pharisees also do the same, but Yours eat and drink." [34]And Jesus said to them, "You cannot make the attendants of the bridegroom fast while the bridegroom is with them, can you? [35]"But *the* days will come; and when the bridegroom is taken away from them, then they will fast in those days."

The Pharisees and the scribes began grumbling that Jesus' disciples (and, by implication, Jesus Himself) were not living up to the standards that they deemed the norm. Their concern was ceremonial cleanness, and the practice of the disciples would render them, according to the interpretation of the Pharisees, unclean. Tax collectors because of their occupations and dealings with Gentiles were unclean. A sinner, someone who did not live up to the standards for ritual purity of the Pharisees, would also be unclean. They believed that Jesus' disciples needed to be rebuked because their eating with these people would make them unclean.

Jesus' answer to their question is easily misunderstood. He replies, "It is not those who are well who need a physician but those who are sick. I have not come to call the righteous but the sinners to repentance." One might be tempted to think that the Pharisees and scribes are "well" and "righteous," despite the number of times that Jesus finds Himself at odds with these people whom He frequently terms hypocrites. Some of the sickest people in the New Testament are Pharisees. For a Pharisee, a sinner is any non-Pharisee, anyone who does not live up to their standards of ritual purity. Jesus answers them, "I didn't come to deal with those who deem themselves to be well, but those who recognize that they are sick. It is those who are sick who need a physician." What Jesus is saying is those who know they need a physician will come to the physician. Those who do not recognize that need will not come. People generally do not go to a doctor and follow a doctor's advice unless they are really sick. The Pharisees and religious leaders of Jesus' day did not see themselves as sick. They patted themselves on the back for their righteous lives. Jesus told them, "I didn't come to deal with you."

These religious leaders move the discussion back to Jesus and His ministry. They say, "Something is wrong with your ministry. You are dealing with the wrong kind of folks. And your disciples have a distorted sense of what holiness is. The disciples of John often fast and offer prayers. The disciples of the Pharisees do the same thing, but your disciples eat and drink." They argued that the problems with Jesus and His ministry were two-fold: first He and His disciples ate and drank with the wrong folks; second they were eating and drinking, instead of fasting and mourning. According to them, something was wrong with Jesus' teaching.

Jesus first responds by calling to mind a normal practice. If one pledged to fast and a wedding feast fell in the middle of that period of fasting, he would simply stop the fast during the wedding feast and pick it up again after the wedding party was over. Jesus told them that is the way it is with His disciples: "You cannot make the attendants of the bridegroom fast while the bridegroom is with them, can you?" The answer that is expected is "Of course not!"

The days will come when the bridegroom is gone, and then they will fast. The same is true with Jesus' disciples. There will be plenty of time for them to mourn and fast when He is taken away from them. Now is not that time.

It is at this point that Jesus illustrates that His ministry is different from the ministry envisioned by religious leaders. The difference is so significant that one cannot just make a few minor adjustments in his or her view of spirituality.

LUKE 5:36

³⁶**And He was also telling them a parable: "No one tears a piece of cloth from a new garment and puts it on an old garment; otherwise he will both tear the new, and the piece from the new will not match the old."**

The parable is best understood by those who remember the days before garments came "preshrunk." You may remember the days of going to school with stiff jeans too long and too big around. When they were washed, they softened, lightened in color, and shrunk to fit. In modern parlance the parable might be told as follows:

Suppose you have a favorite pair of jeans. They fit well and are really soft from wear. Unfortunately those jeans develop a hole in a place that must be patched. No one would cut a piece of denim from a new pair of jeans—no matter how ugly those jeans might be—and sew it on the old jeans. You will have ruined the new pair and will ultimately ruin the old pair because, when they are washed, the new patch will shrink, pucker and tear the old pair.

The accounts of the parable in Matthew and Mark differ slightly. In their accounts, the piece of cloth comes not from a new garment; it is simply a new piece of cloth. The message is the same. Jesus is telling the religious leaders, "The good news of the kingdom is not a simple patch on your understanding and teaching of the law. It is not merely a minor adjustment. To understand it as such would destroy the essence of the kingdom I have been preaching. It would also ruin your 'system.'"

LUKE 5:37-39

³⁷**"And no one puts new wine into old wineskins; otherwise the new wine will burst the skins and it will be spilled out, and the skins will be ruined. ³⁸"But new wine must be put into fresh wineskins. ³⁹"And no one, after drinking old *wine* wishes for new; for he says, 'The old is good *enough*.'"**

At this point Jesus tells a sister parable, the parable of the new wine and an old wineskin. This time the account of the parable in Luke matches the accounts in Matthew and in Mark. In biblical times, people made special containers out of animal skins. They would remove the head, bones, and all the internal organs, sew up any openings, and use one leg as a spout. These skins were then used to store water, wine, and oil. After aging, the skins would lose the pliability and become stiff and hard. If one were to put new wine in old wineskins, as the wine began to ferment, the skin would need to expand. And finally, if an old skin were used, the wineskin would burst. The skins would be ruined; the wine would be spilled and wasted. New wine must be put in fresh wineskins. Everyone in the audience would have known that this was the way it was done. Once the wineskins get old, as almost anyone who has traveled in Palestine can vouch, they become so hard one could almost drive nails with them.

Jesus is again telling His audience, "I didn't come to patch up your old system. I can't put the teaching of the kingdom into your way of doing things. It will never fit into your traditions. To do such will ruin the way you do things, and it would ruin My message. You have misunderstood the nature of My message if you think I came just to patch up the old way of life. We are looking at a significant change."

At this point in Luke, Jesus illustrates why it is that the Pharisees are not willing to come to His message of the kingdom. Why is it that they do not accept the gospel that He preaches to them? Jesus tells them that no one after drinking old wine wants the new. Such a person will simply say, "the old is better." Some translations have "the old is good enough." This verse appears only in Luke's Gospel and is missing in the parallels in Matthew and Mark.

Do you remember the day when Coca-Cola introduced New Coke in an attempt to cut into Pepsi's share of the market? People immediately said, "Don't give us this new sweeter coke. We like the old. It is better. We are used to the old." Coca-Cola found it necessary to bring back the old Coke Classic.

So it was with folks in Jesus day. The Pharisees were saying, "We're used to a system of justification by law, a system where keeping ritual cleanness is the heart of our understanding of the law. That's what really matters to us. We like our old system. You come preaching this new heart-felt religion, and we're not ready for it."

The same was true for those in Luke's day. The Judaizers were used to a system where Gentiles would come to God by going through a system of law keeping, circumcision, and by becoming a proselyte. Now they learned from Paul and others that these Gentiles could accept the gospel and come directly to God. They, like Jewish converts to Christianity, would express their faith in God, be baptized, and become a part of the community of faith.

The struggle has not disappeared with people in our day. If one tries to tell them that the implication of the gospel for people in their era is something different from the way they have always done things, they are resistant to change. Jesus was advocating change based on His understanding of the will of God. Whenever we advocate change, we can still expect people to be hesitant.

LIVING IN GOD'S REIGN

1. The claims of deeds of faith while lives were not obedient was a problem in Jesus' day. How does that apply to our situation today?
2. Believers must still count the cost of being a believer. No matter what deeds are required, salvation is not by deeds. Discuss the relationships among counting the cost, salvation by grace through faith, and obedience.
3. If those who call themselves Christians and claim to be God's children are represented by one sin in the parable of the two sons, who would the other son represent?
4. Discuss the hesitancy many have with regard to change, even when the change can be demonstrated to be an appropriate response to the current culture. How do the parables of the patched garment and the wineskins apply in such a situation?

CHAPTER 12
When God Reigns, More Will Come to Him

Growth of the kingdom in the world is certain, but unfortunately that growth often does not follow the direction believers would choose. Jesus makes a small start, but the kingdom of God will reach out to touch the whole world. Sometimes though there are those who simply do not respond (see the earlier study of the parable of the sower), and on other occasions the growth will be much slower than believers would hope. How should the believer respond to all of this?

Parable of the Mustard Seed

A very short parable appears in Matthew 13, Mark 4, and Luke 13 addressing the amazing growth of the kingdom. We will examine Mark's version of the parable. The parable of the mustard seed appears in the midst of a collection of kingdom parables. Many the parables of this section in Matthew, Mark and Luke deal with the subject of agriculture: the parable of the sower, the parable of the tares (weeds), the parable of the patient farmer, and the parable of the mustard seed.

MARK 4:30-32

[30]And He said, "How shall we picture the kingdom of God, or by what parable shall we present it? [31]*It is* like a mustard seed, which, when sown upon the soil, though it is smaller than all the seeds that are upon the soil, [32]yet when it is sown, it grows up and becomes larger than all the garden plants and forms large branches; so that THE BIRDS OF THE AIR can NEST UNDER ITS SHADE."

Although most often in the parables Jesus uses the word "kingdom" in the sense of God's reign in the individual believer's life, this time He may very well be using it in the sense of the reign of God corporately in His church. The small mustard seed provides a wonderful illustration of the small start for His church—twelve disciples then one hundred and twenty then three thousand and finally the utter most parts of the earth.

On my first trip to Palestine, as I stood outside the traditional site of Lazarus' tomb, I noticed what I thought was a tree. This treelike plant was nearly ten feet tall. On closer examination I saw little yellow blossoms with what looked like tiny black seeds in those blossoms. A Palestinian man stood nearby holding some seeds in his hand and yelling out, "One dollar, one dollar, one dollar." He informed us that he was selling mustard seeds. He hoped that the naive Americans would not know to reach up and gather all the seeds they wanted for free. The mustard seed plant did look like a tree, a big pretty tree with nice yellow blossoms.

This huge plant gets its start as a very small seed. It was the smallest of the seeds that Jews of Jesus' day would plant in their garden. It is not the smallest seed ever. There are those who point to smaller seeds and argue that the Gospels here contain an error. That is not the point Jesus is here trying to make. The mustard seed was the smallest of the seeds that they would sow in their garden. In rabbinic thought, the mustard seed was proverbial for smallness.

Despite the small size of the seed, the plant grows up and becomes larger than all other garden plants. It can have branches large enough that the birds of the air can perch in its branches (Matthew; Luke) or in its shade (Mark).

A frequent Old Testament illustration for the kingdom is a large tree with birds flocking to its branches (Judg. 9:15; Ezek. 17:22-24; 31:3-14; Dan. 4:7-23). In these images, birds are sometimes used to represent the nations, the Gentiles. This could suggest that Jesus intends His audience to see the birds as a reference to the fact that the Gentiles are going to find rest in the kingdom as well. The corporate reign of God, His church, will reach out even to the Gentiles.

The kingdom will have a meager beginning with twelve men. Even the composition of Jesus' twelve disciples would have seemed unlikely to amount to much—fishermen, a tax collector, a rebel, and some other unimportant folks. Although the initial appearance of the kingdom may seem inconsequential, just as tiny seeds lead to huge mature plants, so the kingdom will grow and extend its boundaries. Jesus need not stress the greatness of the future kingdom; few in His day would have disputed that. He instead chose a metaphor to emphasize the kingdom's tiny beginning. These twelve guys are those of whom you would never dream anything important could come. In short order in the book of Acts, the twelve became one hundred twenty, three thousand, five thousand, and then so many they could not be counted.

<u>*Parable of the Yeast*</u>

The next parable is a sister parable to the parable of the mustard seed. It appears only in Matthew and Luke. We will examine Matthew's version of the parable. Again we learn that the kingdom produces ultimate consequences out of all proportion to its insignificant beginnings.

MATTHEW 13:33

³³**He spoke another parable to them, "The kingdom of heaven is like leaven, which a woman took and hid in three pecks of flour until it was all leavened."**

Each time bread was made in biblical times a little pinch of the dough with yeast already at work from a previous batch was saved. The woman in this parable takes a bushel of wheat and puts in that little pinch of dough with the leaven along with some water. Before long the yeast leavens the whole mixture. This woman is going to make a lot of bread. Several cups of flour will make several loaves of bread. This mixture will produce an enormous amount of bread. Despite the attempts of some, there is little merit in trying to identify for what the woman stands, any more than the man in Matthew 13:31.

Although yeast is normally associated with evil in the Old Testament, this is not always so (cf. Lev. 7:13; 23:15-18). If there is a distinction between this parable and the parable of the mustard seed, it would be that the mustard seed indicates massive growth while the yeast indicates intensive internal transformation. Yeast does not grow like the mustard seed; instead it permeates its host. The inevitable effect, despite the small quantity used, is growth and transformation. One may be reminded of Jesus' words in Matthew 5:13 where He uses the metaphor of salt for the kingdom to teach of this transforming power. In both parables it is clear that the kingdom of heaven operates quietly, rather unobtrusively, and from small beginnings. Like the parable of the mustard seed, the point is "little start, big finish." This time, however, there seems to be a special emphasis on the effect—the kingdom will touch everything.

Jesus concludes with another brief discourse on why He uses parables (see chapter 3).

MATTHEW 13:34-35

³⁴**All these things Jesus spoke to the crowds in parables, and He did not speak to them without a parable.** ³⁵***This was* to fulfill what was spoken through the prophet:**

"I WILL OPEN MY MOUTH IN PARABLES;

I WILL UTTER THINGS HIDDEN SINCE THE
FOUNDATION OF THE WORLD."

Matthew informs his readers that Jesus did not speak to the crowds without using parables. This does not mean that He told nothing but parables to the crowd. He does use other teaching methodologies. Rather Matthew is informing them that Jesus always used parables in that mix, He said nothing to them without using parables. Parables were an essential part of Jesus' spoken ministry. Matthew then informs his readers that this was a fulfillment of Scripture, in particular of Psalm 78:2, a psalm of Asaph. The psalm itself was not predictive, but Jesus does fill it full of meaning. Asaph is informing his readers that he has chosen events in their history to bring out things that have been hidden riddles "since the foundation of the world." Similarly Jesus uses parables to proclaim hidden things—the nature of God, the nature of His kingdom, His will for their lives. Note that, unlike Matthew 13:11-17, there is here no emphasis on Jesus' use of parables to keep things hidden. They are to reveal—in conjunction with our earlier exegesis of that text in chapter 3—the message of the kingdom to those who have the right heart to hear.

Parable of the Patient Farmer

The parable of the patient farmer is the only parable unique to Mark's Gospel. It is a simple parable with an important message for the disciples as they begin the work of sharing the gospel.

MARK 4:26-29

   [26]**And He was saying, "The kingdom of God is like a man who casts seed upon the soil; [27]and he goes to bed at night and gets up by day, and the seed sprouts and grows—how, he himself does not know. [28]"The soil produces crops by itself; first the blade, then the head, then the mature grain in the head. [29]"But when the crop permits, he immediately puts in the sickle, because the harvest has come."**

It seems that this parable is given to the twelve (see Mark 4:11; see also Matt. 13:10 for the context of the kingdom parables in this group). It falls right on the heels of Jesus' explanation of the parable of the sower to the twelve. While both this parable and the parable of the sower address the farmer's (sower's) part in planting the seeds, the emphasis here is different. The parable of the sower emphasizes the importance of proper soil for the growth of the seed and an abundant harvest. Here there is an emphasis on the mysterious power in the seed itself and the need for the farmer to patiently await the results of that mysterious power. In both parables the disciples' attitude toward sowing the seed is of vital importance. This time He wants them to realize that they do not produce the result and must simply await God's work through His word.

As in the parable of the mustard seed and the parable of the leaven, this parable relates to the kingdom of God (v. 26) and, more particularly, how that kingdom grows. All the farmer can do is plant the seed on suitable ground. He cannot make the seed grow. He does not even understand how it grows (v. 27). But it does grow, and "all by itself the soil produces grain" (v. 28).

The farmer in this parable does not stand over the seed impatiently urging it to grow. Teachers often give young students an opportunity to have some experience with seeds and plants by letting them plant seeds in little milk cartons, placing the cartons in the classroom window, watering the soil, and waiting for the growth. Each day the children head straight for the window to see if anything has happened. Every day they ask the same question, "Has it grown yet?" Good teachers always pick seeds that sprout very quickly because the children are not very patient.

The farmer recognizes that the growth will not be immediate. He just casts the seed on the soil, goes to bed at night, gets up by day, does his chores everyday, and assumes the seeds will grow. The seed sprouts and grows. He does not understand how it grows. He cannot explain it. But he is patient as he just waits for it to grow. The soil produces the crop all by itself—first the blade, then the head, and then the mature grain. Then comes the harvest.

Jesus has issued a call for those who are involved in the task of sharing the word to remember this parable. As in the parable of the sower, the seed is the word. Jesus is telling the twelve, "Be patient with folks. You simply do what you're supposed to do. You let God do what God does. It is God who gives the growth." One is reminded of the words of Paul in 1 Corinthians 3:7, "So then neither the one who plants nor the one who waters is anything, but God who causes the growth." Growth is slow. Do your job. Be patient. God will give the increase.

Parable of the Tares

Jesus seems to have returned to the crowds, but He provides a parable that seems best intended especially for His disciples. In the midst of the kingdom parables of Matthew 13, there are several parables about farming. Apparently connected with the parable of the sower, Jesus now shares with the twelve the parable of the tares or the weeds. This parable appears only in Matthew. Note that the explanation of the parable is separated by a few verses from the parable itself.

MATTHEW 13:24-30

[24]Jesus presented another parable to them, saying, "The kingdom of heaven may be compared to a man who sowed good seed in his field. [25]"But while his men were sleeping, his enemy came and sowed tares among the wheat, and went away. [26]"But when the wheat sprouted and bore grain, then the tares became evident also. [27]"The slaves of the landowner came and said to him, 'Sir, did you not sow good seed in your field? How then does it have tares?' [28]"And he said to them, 'An enemy has done this!' The slaves *said to him, 'Do you want us, then, to go and gather them up?' [29]"But he *said, 'No; for while you are gathering up the tares, you may uproot the wheat with them. [30]'Allow both to grow together until the harvest; and in the time of the harvest I will say to the reapers, "First gather up the tares and bind them in bundles to burn them up; but gather the wheat into my barn."'"

The parable of sower (Matt. 13:1-9, 18-23; Mark 4:3-8; Luke 8:5-8, 11-15; see also chapter 3 of this book) had shown that although the kingdom will grow amid hard hearts, competing pressures, and even failure, it will produce an abundant crop. The disciples might well ask whether they, as servants of the kingdom, should immediately separate crop from weeds. The temptation for them was to say, "Let's pull up these weeds, get rid of all wicked people, kill all the heretics." This parable answers that question with a resounding "No!" There will be a delay in separation until the harvest.

The text tells us that Jesus "told" (literally, "set another before them") another parable. The "them" is apparently the crowd and not the disciples (cf. vv. 34, 36). It is again important to point out that Jesus is not saying that the kingdom of heaven is "like a man who . . . ," but rather the kingdom of heaven is like the story He is telling, "like the situation of man who. . . ." While his servants are sleeping in creeps the enemy. "Sleeping" here does not indicate that the servants were neglectful. Rather the implication is that the enemy was sneaky and malicious.

The enemy sows tares (NIV "weeds") in the man's field. The Greek word indicates bearded darnel (*lolium temulentum*). Botanically, this plant is very close to wheat and very difficult to distinguish from the wheat when the plants are young. This weed apparently bore bacteria that were poisonous to livestock. Apparently it was not at all unusual for people to do such a dastardly deed as a way of getting even. In fact, in the ancient Near East there were laws written against such a deed, and there was even a particular curse in the rabbinic literature placed upon someone who would do this to his neighbor.

The roots of the two plants entangled themselves around one another. As soon as the heads of grain began to appear on the wheat, there was no doubt which plant was which. The wheat would ripen with yellow heads while the tares were a charcoal gray. The Greek indicates that the enemy sowed the tares "among the wheat," indicating in the original a thorough distribution of those bad seeds.

When it becomes clear to the servants that tares have been sown among the wheat, they tell the master about the weeds. They ask what seems to be a foolish question, "Sir, didn't you sow good seed in your field? How then does it have tares?" Of course, he did not sow tares. No one would do such a thing. The owner immediately blames an enemy. They ask the master, "Should we pull up those weeds now that they are becoming clear?" But the master forbids his servants from separating the tares from the wheat until the harvest. At that time the reapers will gather the tares—weeds seem always to grow taller than the crops we intend to plant. These weeds will be so plentiful that they will be gathered up and burned. The master has chosen one of the two common practices to get rid of such weeds: either the women and children are given the task of flicking out the weeds or the reapers pull them together first before harvesting the good grain.

The "harvest" is a common metaphor for final judgment. Unlike the parable of the sower (vv. 19-23), in this parable the "good seed" (v. 24) is not the "word" or the "message." It is rather good people ready to face the final judgment.

Jesus is informing His hearers that the kingdom can be present in the world while not ridding the world of all evil. They may have expected the kingdom to simply eradicate all bad. They must wait until the harvest. It is not until later in the chapter that Jesus provides His interpretation of the parable.

MATTHEW 13:36-43

³⁶Then He left the crowds and went into the house. And His disciples came to Him and said, "Explain to us the parable of the tares of the field." ³⁷And He said, "The one who sows the good seed is the Son of Man, ³⁸and the field is the world; and *as for* the good seed, these are the sons of the kingdom; and the tares are the sons of the evil *one*; ³⁹and the enemy who sowed them is the devil, and the harvest is the end of the age; and the reapers are angels. ⁴⁰"So just as the tares are gathered up and burned with fire, so shall it be at the end of the age. ⁴¹"The Son of Man will send forth His angels, and they will gather out of His kingdom all stumbling blocks, and those who commit lawlessness, ⁴²and will throw them into the furnace of fire; in that place there will

be weeping and gnashing of teeth. ⁴³Then THE RIGHTEOUS WILL
SHINE FORTH AS THE SUN in the kingdom of their Father. He who
has ears, let him hear."

Jesus leaves the crowd and returns to the house, perhaps the house of
Peter in Capernaum. The disciples, like with the parable of the sower, discover they need an explanation. They are not brighter than the crowds; they simply have the sense and the close association with Jesus that allows them to ask
for an explanation.

Jesus explicitly tells the disciples that the "field is the world." Many have suggested that the field should be seen as the church, indicating an assembly composed of both faithful, good Christians and those who are not true to Jesus. That
does not, however, fit Jesus' own words. It would seem that the problem Jesus
foresees is the fact that the kingdom does not totally transform the world. Notice
that Jesus' statement here presupposes a mission that goes beyond Israel.

It is important to see that it is for the sake of the good plants that the tares
are not immediately uprooted, and again at the "harvest" it is for their sake
that the tares will be destroyed. The weeds are "the sons of the evil one"; the
devil himself has had the bad seed sown. The harvest is the end of the age, and
the harvesters are the angels of God. This parable, like the parable of the
sower, has many allegorical elements without being a full-fledged allegory. The
elements, though, arise from the context and are not left to the imagination
of the interpreter.

Just as the tares are gathered up and burned with fire, the same thing will
happen to the sons of the evil one at the end of the age. The Son of Man will
send His angels to gather out of His kingdom all stumbling blocks, and those
who commit lawlessness. Such will be thrown into the furnace of fire where
there will be weeping and gnashing of teeth. Jesus proclaims a contrast between
the sons of the evil one and the sons of the kingdom, the righteous. The righteous "will shine forth as the sun," an allusion to Daniel 12:3. Jesus concludes
as He has earlier parables with the admonition, "He who has ears, let him hear."

Jesus is telling His disciples that it is not their job to be the judges. They
are simply to spread the message, allow growth to occur, and allow those at
the end time to do the judging. In the Sermon on the Mount, Jesus had
already taught the danger of judging/condemning.

MATTHEW 7:1-5

¹"Do not judge so that you will not be judged. ²"For in the
way you judge, you will be judged; and by your standard of measure, it will be measured to you. ³"Why do you look at the speck

that is in your brother's eye, but do not notice the log that is in your own eye? ⁴"Or how can you say to your brother, 'Let me take the speck out of your eye,' and behold, the log is in your own eye? ⁵"You hypocrite, first take the log out of your own eye, and then you will see clearly to take the speck out of your brother's eye."

The believer does not have all the necessary information to serve as judge. He cannot see motives; he may not understand circumstances. He may think he is pulling up a weed only to discover it was a shaft of wheat. In aggressively going after the weeds, he may pull up the good plants at the same time. We are often asked, "Will folks who do a, b or c go to heaven or hell?" Our answer should be, "That's God's business. I don't make heaven and hell judgments." It is by God's grace that anyone is saved. Will God understandingly say, "Well, they didn't know better"? We do not know. We have a just and fair, honest and loving God. He will always do the right thing. Allow God to do the judging.

Parable of the Dragnet

The next parable, the parable of the dragnet, also appears only in Matthew. It is a sister parable to the parable of the tares with a similar meaning. The parable of tares focuses on a period of time while the reign of God on earth is prospering before the judgment, during which time the tares coexist with the wheat. The parable of the net simply jumps to the situation at the Last Judgment. The advent of the kingdom embraces both "good" fish and "bad" fish, and only a final sweep through the net will sort them out.

MATTHEW 13:47-50

⁴⁷"Again, the kingdom of heaven is like a dragnet cast into the sea, and gathering *fish* of every kind; ⁴⁸and when it was filled, they drew it up on the beach; and they sat down and gathered the good *fish* into containers, but the bad they threw away. ⁴⁹"So it will be at the end of the age; the angels will come forth and take out the wicked from among the righteous, ⁵⁰and will throw them into the furnace of fire; in that place there will be weeping and gnashing of teeth."

The dragnet (a word used only here in the New Testament) was pulled along between two boats or tied somewhere on shore at one end while the other end was taken out by a boat. Both ends of the net were then drawn to land by ropes. Although some have suggested that "fish of every kind" might refer to the fact that Christianity would cross all racial boundaries, verse 48 makes it clear that Jesus is referring to "good" and "bad" fish. In the parable, "good" and "bad" fish do not indicate anything of the moral nature of the fish. It is simply used by Jesus to refer to fish that met the Old Testament rules for ritual purity (Lev. 11:9-12). When one is fishing, he cannot swerve the net around to miss the bad fish and catch only the good ones. He simply catches whatever he catches and sorts them out only when they have been brought to land.

The parable, like the parable of the tares, clearly points to the Last Judgment. The angels again do the separating, and the end for the bad fish, like for the tares, is a fiery furnace.

Both the parable of the tares and the parable of the dragnet call disciples to leave the judging to God. They lack the necessary discernment to tell the good from the bad; in trying to avoid catching a bad fish, they may miss a good fish. The believer's task is to plant the good seed and to go fishing.

Jesus concludes the parables of Matthew 13 with a question and an illustration:

MATTHEW 13:51-52

[51]**"Have you understood all these things?" They said to Him, "Yes."**

[52]**And Jesus said to them, "Therefore every scribe who has become a disciple of the kingdom of heaven is like a head of a household, who brings out of his treasure things new and old."**

Jesus had explained two parables in chapter 13 in depth. Have His disciples caught on to this way of teaching? Are they getting His message?

Jesus then gives an illustration to help them see that to be a student of the Old Testament is not an obstacle but a blessing for the one who understands and accepts the nature of the kingdom. He tells them that a scribe who has become a disciple of the kingdom of heaven is like a head of a household who brings out of his treasure things that are old and things that are new. Scribes spent their lives copying the Scriptures. In so doing they became experts in the Old Testament. They were the great teachers of the day. Such people were not at a disadvantage when it comes to the kingdom of God. They understood the message of the old covenant. Now as disciples of the kingdom they understand the message of Jesus. They can see how it all fits together, how Jesus fulfills (fills full of meaning of) the Law. Later the Apostle Paul, although a trained rabbi, becomes a great teacher and will bring out things old and new.

LIVING IN GOD'S REIGN

1. Does the initial smallness of the church's beginning and the way it ultimately touches the world provide any evidence regarding God's work?
2. Why is patience with new converts and patience with a growing local church such a problem for believers? Discuss how the parable of the patient farmer addresses this situation.
3. How should a realization that God, not the preacher or for that matter any Christian, produces growth affect evangelistic efforts?
4. What are the implications of the parable of the tares and the parable of the dragnet for a judgmental spirit? How can we change the way many in the world have viewed Christians in this regard?

CHAPTER 13
God's Reign and Judgment

Several of the parables already studied have implications for eschatology (a study of last times) and the judgment—the rich man and Lazarus, the talents, the minas, the tares, and the dragnet. Although the final judgment and the fall of Jerusalem may seem disconnected to the modern reader, for the original readers the connection was clear. Both were times of God's intervention. Both represented a day of the Lord. This chapter will examine parables that deal with the fall of Jerusalem and the final judgment.

Parable of the Weather

Telling the weather in Palestine is much easier than it is in most of the United States. Their rainy season is November through January. Some later rains come in March or April. The rest of the year one could count on it being dry. Jesus tells His audience that they can predict the weather, but seem to be missing the clear evidence of what is about to happen.

MATTHEW 16:1-4

¹The Pharisees and Sadducees came up, and testing Jesus, they asked Him to show them a sign from heaven. ²But He replied to them, "When it is evening, you say, '*It will be* fair weather, for the sky is red.' ³"And in the morning, '*There will be* a storm today, for the sky is red and threatening.' Do you know how to discern the appearance of the sky, but cannot *discern* the signs of the times? ⁴"An evil and adulterous generation seeks after a sign; and a sign will not be given it, except the sign of Jonah." And He left them and went away.

It is amazing that, despite all the miracles Jesus has performed, the Pharisees and Sadducees come asking for another sign. The fact that a single article ("the") is used to describe both groups indicates that they were, despite political and religious differences, working in tandem. They wanted some definitive sign that would demonstrate who Jesus was and put aside all doubts.

Jesus has just fed 5,000, healed masses of sick people, and fed 4,000. For these religious leaders, those are magic tricks that indicate nothing. They have come to put Jesus to the test.

Jesus responds to their request by reciting a proverb. We are more familiar with a modern version of the proverb, "Red sky at morning, sailor take warning. Red sky at night, sailor's delight." Jesus is referring to a similar adage in His day. He tells these leaders that it is amazing that they can read the signs in the skies and predict the weather but cannot read the signs around them. The signs point to Jesus and the dawning of the kingdom. Jesus has said and done things that clearly indicate the advent of the kingdom predicted in their Scriptures. The coming of the kingdom and the fall of their nation should be clear. Yet despite all the signs, they have missed what God is doing and is about to do.

Jesus describes them as a wicked and adulterous generation. They have seen the signs Jesus has already performed but are looking for some other special miraculous sign. Jesus says that none will be given except the sign of Jonah. When Jonah came to Nineveh, he performed no miracles. Those pagans at Nineveh responded. Here Jews, with all of the evidence, fail to respond. If Jesus is alluding to the sign of "three days and three nights in the belly of the fish" as He does elsewhere (Matt. 12:20), that is not clear here.

Those with eyes to see can already see the signs of the times.

Parable of the Fig Tree and Its Leaves

The parable of the fig tree and its leaves appears in both Matthew 24:32-35 and Mark 13:28-32. The context for the parable begins at the beginning of Matthew 24 with Jesus and the disciples viewing the temple from the Mount of Olives.

MATTHEW 24:1-3

¹Jesus came out from the temple and was going away when His disciples came up to point out the temple buildings to Him. ²And He said to them, "Do you not see all these things? Truly I say to you, not one stone here will be left upon another, which will not be torn down." ³As He was sitting on the Mount of Olives, the disciples came to Him privately, saying, "Tell us, when will these things happen, and what *will be* the sign of Your coming, and of the end of the age?"

Jesus' prediction of the fall of Jerusalem and the destruction of the temple leads His disciples to ask three questions: 1) "when will these things happen," 2) "and what *will be* the sign of Your coming," 3) "and of the end of the age?" Carson summarizes the situation well:

> "The *disciples* think of Jerusalem's destruction and the eschatological end as a single complex web of events. This accounts for the form of their questions. Jesus warns that there will be delay *before* the End—a delay characterized by persecution and tribulation for his followers (vv. 42-8), but with one particularly violent display of judgment in the Fall of Jerusalem (vv. 15-21; Mark 13:14-20; Luke 21:20-24). Immediately after the days of that sustained persecution . . . comes the Second Advent."[27]

Although there has been significant debate about the material in Matthew 24, it seems reasonable that Jesus would answer the disciples' questions. The real difficulty rests in knowing which question Jesus is answering. It is interesting that the second coming and the fall of Jerusalem are discussed in the same chapter and that the language used to discuss each is similar.

Verses 4 through 28 address the fall of Jerusalem. Jesus warns of false Messiahs, persecution, the desolation of the holy place, and hardships that will come with fleeing from the city. It seems that Jesus is making a transition in verse 29 when He says, "But immediately after the tribulation of those days. . . ." The real issue is the phrase, "those days." Jesus has consistently used that phrase in this text to refer to the fall of Jerusalem. If that be the case, then verse 29 may provide the transition to the discussion of the second coming. Immediately after the fall of Jerusalem,

MATTHEW 24:29-31

[29]". . . THE SUN WILL BE DARKENED, AND THE MOON WILL NOT GIVE ITS LIGHT, AND THE STARS WILL FALL from the sky, and the powers of the heavens will be shaken. [30]"And then the sign of the Son of Man will appear in the sky, and then all the tribes of the earth will mourn, and they will see the SON OF MAN COMING ON THE CLOUDS OF THE SKY with power and great glory. [31]"And He will send forth His angels with A GREAT TRUMPET and THEY WILL GATHER TOGETHER His elect from the four winds, from one end of the sky to the other."

---

[27] D.A. Carson, *Matthew*, Expositor's Bible Commentary (Grand Rapids: Zondervan, 1976), p. 495.

Here the matter under discussion seems clearly to be the second coming of Jesus. But, the next paragraph, the parable of the fig tree, seems to jump back to a discussion of the fall of Jerusalem. It is significant that the fall of Jerusalem is the event that must occur before the second coming.

MATTHEW 24:32-35

[32]"Now learn the parable from the fig tree: when its branch has already become tender and puts forth its leaves, you know that summer is near; [33]so, you too, when you see all these things, recognize that He is near, *right* at the door. [34]"Truly I say to you, this generation will not pass away until all these things take place. [35]"Heaven and earth will pass away, but My words will not pass away."

Fig trees leaf out and bear fruit late. In fact, it is often June before the trees get their leaves. They are the last of the trees in Palestine to get their leaves. When the leaves are on the fig trees, then one knows that summer is just around the corner.

The real difficulty in interpreting this section rests on how one is to understand the phrase "all these things" in verses 33 and 34. If one includes celestial signs and Parousia (the second coming) itself (vv. 29-31), then verses 32-33 would be problematic, because any distinction between "all these things" and "it is near" would be destroyed. It is more natural to take "all these things" as referring to the distress of verses 4-28. The tribulation will come on believers throughout period between Jesus' ascension and His return.

Jesus is here making two points. First, "all these things" (vv. 4-28) must happen; and then the Parousia (the second coming) is "near, right at the door, imminent." The second coming will be the next major step in God's redemptive purposes. Second, all of this does not mean that by observing the period of distress one can pinpoint the Parousia, for Jesus has said "no one knows about that day or hour" (vv. 36-42).

Jesus begins His discourse in verse 34 with "Truly I say to you" or "I tell you the truth" emphasizing the importance of what He is about to say. "This generation" refers to the generation living when Jesus spoke. It is, to say the least, problematic to assume that Jesus mistakenly thought the Parousia would occur within His hearers' lifetime. If our interpretation of this chapter is right, all that verse 34 demands is that the distress of verses 4-28, including Jerusalem's fall, must happen within the lifetime of the generation then living. It does *not* mean that the distress must end within that time but only that "all these things" must happen within it. Everything necessary for the second coming, including the fall of Jerusalem, must happen within a generation of

AD 30. But there is no firm date for the second coming itself; "only the Father" knows when it will happen (v. 36). Jesus goes on to say that the authority and eternal validity of His words are nothing less than the authority and eternal validity of God's words (see Ps. 119:89-90; Isa. 40:6-8).

Jesus is then telling His disciples, "If you've been watching the things I have told you, you will know when Jerusalem will fall and sometime after that will come My return." Jesus informs the disciples that they cannot know the hour nor the day of the second coming (vv. 36-41).

Notice that the fall of Jerusalem and the second coming are both "a day of the Lord." As for the fall of Jerusalem, Jesus says, "He is near, right at the door." God will enter their history and intervene. Jesus then concludes with these words, "This generation shall not pass away until all these things take place." If Jesus were referring to the end of time, the second coming, He was obviously wrong. If, however, the issue is the fall of Jerusalem, then indeed many standing there on that day would see that event.

Parable of the Watchful Servant

The title "the watchful servant" is a bit more descriptive of the version of the parable in Mark 13:32-37 than the one in Luke 12:35-38. In Mark, each of the servants receives an assignment from his master before the master leaves on a journey. The doorkeeper is to keep watch. All of the servants are to keep watch since they do not know the time when the owner of the house will return. The master goes away apparently to another country. The master may return "in the evening, or at midnight, or when the rooster crows, or at dawn."

In Luke's parable, all of the servants are to be ready to open the door when the master returns from a wedding banquet on a given night. Luke's parable might better be termed "the waiting servants." Although Mark may divide the night into four watches following the Roman custom, Luke divides the night into three watches.

MARK 13:33-37

³³"Take heed, keep on the alert; for you do not know when the *appointed* time will come. ³⁴"*It is* like a man away on a journey, *who* upon leaving his house and putting his slaves in charge, *assigning* to each one his task, also commanded the doorkeeper to stay on the alert. ³⁵"Therefore, be on the alert—for you do not know when the master of the house is coming, whether in the evening, at midnight, or when the rooster crows, or in the morning—³⁶in case he should come suddenly and find you asleep. ³⁷"What I say to you I say to all, 'Be on the alert!'"

Each servant is given an appropriate task to accomplish while the master is away on a journey. The watchman is given the task of watching the entrance to the estate. He is responsible for the ultimate security of all who are within the house. The master may return at any time. The NIV similarly records Jesus' statement as offering four possible times of return—"in the evening, or at midnight, or when the rooster crows, or at dawn." Mark may be suggesting the Roman procedure of dividing the night into four three-hour watch shifts—six to nine, nine to midnight, midnight to three, three to six.

It is interesting that the tasks assigned the other slaves seem less interesting or important than the task given the doorkeeper. Jesus is exhorting His disciples to be vigilant. No one can ascertain the exact time of His return.

LUKE 12:35-38

35"Be dressed in readiness, and *keep* your lamps lit. 36"Be like men who are waiting for their master when he returns from the wedding feast, so that they may immediately open *the door* to him when he comes and knocks. 37"Blessed are those slaves whom the master will find on the alert when he comes; truly I say to you, that he will gird himself *to serve*, and have them recline *at the table*, and will come up and wait on them. 38"Whether he comes in the second watch, or even in the third, and finds *them* so, blessed are those *slaves*."

Jesus tells His disciples to be dressed and in readiness, to keep their lamps lit, and to be like men who are waiting for their master when he returns so that they may immediately open the door to him when he comes and knocks. In this parable the master has gone off to a wedding feast. Wedding feasts in biblical times would typically last a long time, perhaps even a week. The servants do not know exactly when their master will return. Jesus proclaims those who are ready and waiting to be "blessed," a term used by Jesus in the beatitudes meaning perhaps "to be congratulated."

When the master comes, he does the unthinkable. He girds himself to serve them. One is immediately reminded of what Jesus does for the twelve in John 13:1-17. The master will have his slaves recline at table. In the culture of the day, that would never happen. It's an amazing event.

Notice that the master's return may come at a time one would not expect, at the second or third watch. In the Jewish world the night was divided into three watches from sunset to sunrise—six to ten, ten to two, two to six. The slaves are to be ready no matter what the hour. So Christians are to be ready and waiting when the Son of Man returns.

Parable of the Thief at Night

The parable of the thief at night follows the parable of the waiting servants in Luke (Luke 12:39-40) and follows an admonition to "keep watch" preceding the parable of the servant entrusted with authority in Matthew (Matt. 24:42-44). Because if its brevity, this parable is often considered a parabolic saying rather than a true parable.

LUKE 12:39-40

³⁹"But be sure of this, that if the head of the house had known at what hour the thief was coming, he would not have allowed his house to be broken into. ⁴⁰"You too, be ready; for the Son of Man is coming at an hour that you do not expect."

The point here is that folks would all repent, or at least offer some pretense of repentance, if they understood the significance of the Lord's return and knew the exact hour. We must be ready for the second coming. It is significant that the New Testament never exhorts Christians to get ready for the Lord's return, but rather to be ready.

Parable of the Steward Entrusted with Authority

The parable of the steward entrusted with authority is another parable where Jesus teaches the necessity of being watchful. In this parable, however, Jesus also stresses faithfulness. In both Matthew 24:45-51 and Luke 12:41-46, Jesus addresses the parable to the disciples. In Matthew, the parable falls in a whole chapter addressing the second coming and follows the parable of the thief. In Luke, however, we gain some helpful additional information. Other than some minor differences in wording, the two accounts of the parable are alike.

LUKE 12:41-46

⁴¹Peter said, "Lord, are You addressing this parable to us, or to everyone *else* as well?" ⁴²And the Lord said, "Who then is the faithful and sensible steward, whom his master will put in charge of his servants, to give them their rations at the proper time? ⁴³"Blessed is that slave whom his master finds so doing when he comes. ⁴⁴"Truly I say to you that he will put him in charge of all his possessions. ⁴⁵"But if that slave says in his heart, 'My master will be a long time in coming,' and begins to beat the slaves, *both* men and women, and to eat and drink and get

drunk; [46]the master of that slave will come on a day when he
does not expect *him* and at an hour he does not know, and will
cut him in pieces, and assign him a place with the unbelievers."

Immediately following the parable of the watchful servants and the parable of the thief, Peter asks a question that elicits this parable. Peter had listened
intently to the parable of the watchful servants. He was uncertain about Jesus'
intended audience in the parable of the watchful servants. Peter asks, "Lord,
are you addressing this parable to us or to everyone else as well?" In other
words, "Who do you have in mind in this parable? Are we the ones who are
to be watchful or does this parable address everyone?"

The answer Jesus provides in the parable of the steward is basically, "It's
especially for you. Those who have more privileges have more responsibilities,
and you, My inner circle, are in that category." The steward, that is, the slave
placed in charge, might begin to think that his master will be a long time in coming and feel that he would be safe in doing whatever he would like. He might
then begin to beat and abuse the other slaves, and to eat and to drink and get
drunk. The master of that slave will come at a time he does not expect and will
punish him appropriately. Jesus describes the punishment as being cut into pieces
and assigned to a place with the unbelievers. We might paraphrase "cut him to
pieces" as "skin him alive." Jesus goes on to warn that that slave who knew his
master's will and did not get ready or act according to his will would receive
many lashes. On the other hand, the one who did not know the master's will
and committed deeds worthy of flogging will receive only a few lashes. Jesus says
the reason for such proportional punishment is that everyone who has been
given much or entrusted with much will have much required of him.

One of the sections of this parable that poses a difficulty with many is the
"many lashes, few lashes." Is Jesus teaching degrees of hell? The real point of
Jesus in the parable is not degrees of hell but degrees of responsibility. The
more one knows and the more one is blessed, the more responsible he is, and
God will judge accordingly.

Jesus' answer to Peter's question is "The parable about the watching slaves
applies to everyone, but it applies especially to you. You have been blessed by
being My disciples. You have learned the mysteries others long to learn. You
especially must act responsibly." The disciples could easily have taken advantage of their positions. When Jesus did not return immediately, it would have
been easy to use their role as His stewards to take advantage of other
Christians. They especially must be watchful.

Parable of the Ten Virgins

The parable of the ten virgins fits well into the sequence of parables appearing in Matthew 24-25. The first parable (24:42-44), the parable of the thief, warns of the unexpectedness of Messiah's coming. The second (24:45-51), the parable of the steward entrusted with authority, shows that more than passive watchfulness is required; one must act according to the master's will and discharge the allotted responsibilities. This third parable (25:1-13), the parable of the virgins, stresses the need for preparedness in the face of an unexpectedly long delay. It is followed by the parable of the talents (25:14-30) which calls for the disciple to use what God has given him.

MATTHEW 25:1-13

[1]"Then the kingdom of heaven will be comparable to ten virgins, who took their lamps and went out to meet the bridegroom. [2]"Five of them were foolish, and five were prudent. [3]"For when the foolish took their lamps, they took no oil with them, [4]but the prudent took oil in flasks along with their lamps. [5]"Now while the bridegroom was delaying, they all got drowsy and *began* to sleep. [6]"But at midnight there was a shout, 'Behold, the bridegroom! Come out to meet *him*.' [7]"Then all those virgins rose and trimmed their lamps. [8]"The foolish said to the prudent, 'Give us some of your oil, for our lamps are going out.' [9]"But the prudent answered, 'No, there will not be enough for us and you *too*; go instead to the dealers and buy *some* for yourselves.' [10]"And while they were going away to make the purchase, the bridegroom came, and those who were ready went in with him to the wedding feast; and the door was shut. [11]"Later the other virgins also came, saying, 'Lord, lord, open up for us.' [12]"But he answered, 'Truly I say to you, I do not know you.' [13]"Be on the alert then, for you do not know the day nor the hour."

The idea of the Messiah as bridegroom is really nothing new. Several Old Testament passages have similar imagery (Isa. 54:46; 62:45; Ezek. 16:7-34; Hos. 2:19). In those passages Yahweh is portrayed as the "husband" of His people. In His parables, Jesus frequently places Himself in Yahweh's place. Both John the Baptist (John 3:27-30) and Jesus (Matt. 9:15; Mark 2:19-20) have already made the equation Jesus = Messiah = bridegroom.

The setting for this parable is fairly typical for the marriage customs of the day. Normally the bridegroom, with some close friends, would leave his home to go to the bride's home. At her home there would be various ceremonies. After those events there would be a procession through the streets, usually after nightfall, to his home.

The ten virgins may have been bridesmaids who had been assisting the bride. They apparently expected to meet the groom as he came from the bride's house to share in the wedding banquet. Everyone in the procession was expected to carry his or her own torch. Anyone without a torch would be assumed to be an uninvited party crasher. The wedding banquet itself might last several days and would be held at the groom's house.

Notice that the bride is not mentioned in the best manuscripts of the parable. She is simply not an essential part of the story for Jesus' point.

There is no significance to the girls being termed virgins or to there being ten of them (simply a favorite, fairly large round number). The word "lamps" here refers either to small clay oil-fed lamps or possibly to torches whose rags would need periodic dowsing with oil to keep them burning. In either case it would be wise to plan ahead and bring along a flask with an additional supply of oil.

Five of the virgins were foolish and five were prudent or wise, a word used in the parable of the dishonest steward (see chapter 8). It here, as there, indicates one who is prudent or shrewd and has planned ahead. The only distinction between the two groups is that the wise bring an extra supply in separate jars, while the foolish bring no extra oil. The wise are prepared for a possible delay; the foolish expect to meet the groom, but are unprepared if there is any delay.

Jesus informs His audience that the bridegroom is a long time coming. At midnight "the cry rang out" (NIV). All the virgins woke up and trimmed their lamps, but the lamps of the foolish virgins quickly went out. There have been numerous attempts to resort to allegorizing the text and making the oil "grace" (many Reformers and later Matthew Henry) or "good works" (Catholic exegetes in response to the Reformers). There is no point in trying to see some hidden meanings in the oil or sleep.

The wise or prudent virgins cannot help the foolish virgins. They either **will not** or **may not** have enough oil. The foresight and preparedness of the wise virgins cannot help the foolish virgins. Being prepared cannot be transferred or shared.

The bridegroom comes, the wise virgins enter, and the door is shut. Despite the intense cries of the ill-prepared and foolish latecomers—"Lord! Lord!"—they remain outside. The parable is about the rejection of those who, despite all appearances and claims, never made preparation for the coming of the kingdom.

Jesus closes the parable by reiterating the central theme: "Be on the alert then, for you do not know the day nor the hour." Interestingly enough, both the wise and the foolish virgins fell asleep. The call of Jesus is not "Stay awake!"

but "Keep watch!" His concern is that they be prepared.

Parable of the Sheep and Goats

Strictly speaking, the next passage is not a parable. It does have parabolic elements—the shepherd, the sheep, the goats, and the actual separation. The parable of the sheep and goats (Matt. 25:31-46) follows the parable of the talents (see chapter 9), and falls in the larger context of several second coming/last days parables.

MATTHEW 25:31-46

[31]"But when the Son of Man comes in His glory, and all the angels with Him, then He will sit on His glorious throne. [32]"All the nations will be gathered before Him; and He will separate them from one another, as the shepherd separates the sheep from the goats; [33]and He will put the sheep on His right, and the goats on the left. [34]"Then the King will say to those on His right, 'Come, you who are blessed of My Father, inherit the kingdom prepared for you from the foundation of the world. [35]"For I was hungry, and you gave Me *something* to eat; I was thirsty, and you gave Me *something* to drink; I was a stranger, and you invited Me in; [36]naked, and you clothed Me; I was sick, and you visited Me; I was in prison, and you came to Me.' [37]"Then the righteous will answer Him, 'Lord, when did we see You hungry, and feed You, or thirsty, and give You *something* to drink? [38]'And when did we see You a stranger, and invite You in, or naked, and clothe You? [39]'When did we see You sick, or in prison, and come to You?' [40]"The King will answer and say to them, 'Truly I say to you, to the extent that you did it to one of these brothers of Mine, *even* the least *of them,* you did it to Me.' [41]"Then He will also say to those on His left, 'Depart from Me, accursed ones, into the eternal fire which has been prepared for the devil and his angels; [42]for I was hungry, and you gave Me *nothing* to eat; I was thirsty, and you gave Me nothing to drink; [43]I was a stranger, and you did not invite Me in; naked, and you did not clothe Me; sick, and in prison, and you did not visit Me.' [44]"Then they themselves also will answer, 'Lord, when did we see You hungry, or thirsty, or a stranger, or naked, or sick, or in prison, and did not take care of You?' [45]"Then He will answer them, 'Truly I say to you, to the extent that you did not do it to one of the least of these, you did not do it to Me.' [46]"These will go away into eternal punishment, but the righteous into eternal life."

These words are spoken by the Lord *only three days before His sufferings.* One of the problems in our text is who are "the least of these my brothers"? The majority of scholars understand "the least of these brothers of mine" to refer to all who are hungry, distressed, and needy. Response to these people then becomes the basis of acceptance into kingdom and is established by deeds of mercy and compassion. The difficulty with this position is that Jesus never elsewhere identifies the least of his brothers with the poor and needy without some distinction. For Jesus, the "least of the brothers" normally refers to the apostles, other Christian missionaries, or sometimes just His disciples. The treatment of these believers and ambassadors of the gospel determines the fate of all men. Because of this, it is probably best to see Jesus' "brothers" as His disciples (see Matt. 12:48-49; 23:8; 28:10). The fate of the nations will be determined by how they respond to Jesus' followers, "missionaries" or not, who have been charged with spreading the gospel in the face of hunger, thirst, illness, and imprisonment.

Good deeds done to Jesus' followers, even the least of them, are not just works of compassion and morality. They reflect where people stand in relation to kingdom and to Jesus Himself. Jesus identifies Himself with the fate of His followers; compassion for them is equal to compassion for Jesus.

Jesus tells His disciples that the Son of Man is going to come, sit on His glorious throne with His angels, and separate the sheep from the goats. In biblical times, as in Palestine today, it was normal to have sheep and goats grazing together. The goats would protect the sheep. Sheep were not fighters; goats were fighters. At night they were often separated. The sheep with all their wool could better tolerate the cool air. The goats would often be herded together for warmth. In sparse grazing areas the animals might be separated during the day as well. The goats could manage on almost anything. When it came time for shearing, one had to separate the animals. The goats' hair was not like wool and was not valued as much.

It is significant that those from all the nations will be gathered to be judged. The sheep are placed on the right, the place of power and honor, and the goats on the left.

In verse 34, Jesus makes a transition from "Son of Man" to "King." That is not at all surprising (cf. Dan. 7:13-14). He addresses the sheep, "Come, you who are blessed by my Father." This time the word "blessed" is not the word used in the beatitudes, which means "to be congratulated." It is rather the word that means "praised" (cf. our word "eulogized"). They now take their inheritance that God prepared for them from "the foundation of the world." This inheritance, the consummated kingdom, was God's plan for those who faithfully responded to the work of His Son from the beginning. The reason they are welcomed and invited to take their inheritance is that they have served the King. It is significant that their service is more evidential than causative for their admission to the kingdom. It is clear that they belong because they have done these deeds. The righteous are a bit surprised. They have not seen their deeds "to the least of the King's brothers" as meritorious or as equivalent to doing the deeds to or for Him. Likely from the context the hungry, thirsty, strangers, naked, sick, and in prison are the believers who have suffered such for their faith. They may even be the traveling missionaries who share the message of the kingdom. Service to those who are His disciples, though they are the world's underdogs, is service to Jesus. The sheep are the people whose work demonstrates that they have responded properly to the King's messengers and, therefore, to the message.

The condemnation of the goats is terrible; they are cursed, banished from the King's presence, and sent to the eternal fire of hell. Hell is here described in categories very familiar to Jews. The kingdom was prepared for the righteous. Hell, while prepared for the devil and his angels, now also serves as the doom of those guilty of failing to show compassion for the least of the King's brothers.

The text paints real concern for the underdogs and the persecuted. It also calls believers to demonstrate Christ's lordship in their lives through acts of service—service to all those who are needy, but especially to the household of faith (Gal. 6:10).

LIVING IN GOD'S REIGN

1. What is the significance of the fact that Christians are never exhorted "to *get* ready" for the Lord's return, but always "to *be* ready"?
2. What is the danger when those in leadership positions in the church do not take the second coming seriously?
3. With privilege comes responsibility. There is always a danger that those in leadership can take advantage of those whom they lead. How can this happen in a church? How can it be avoided?
4. Evaluate the following proverb based on the parable of the wise and foolish virgins: "You cannot rely on someone else's merits. You must be prepared yourself."
5. Who are those Jesus would term "the least of these My brothers"?

ABOUT THE AUTHOR

Dr. Michael Moss is a professor of Bible and Greek at Lipscomb University. He serves there as associate dean of the College of Bible and Ministry and directs the University's graduate Bible program. He also serves as the pulpit minister of the Central Church of Christ in Nashville.

He is the author of numerous book reviews in *Restoration Quarterly* and *Stone-Campbell Journal*; translator, *The NKJV Greek English Interlinear New Testament*, Thomas Nelson, 1994; author, *1, 2 Timothy and Titus*, College Press New International Commentary, College Press, 1994; "The Exposition of Scripture," *Man of God*, Gospel Advocate,1996; *Lord! Sometimes I Don't Feel Saved*, Covenant Publishing, 2002.

Dr. Moss and his wife, Virginia, have three daughters and five grandchildren.

BIBLIOGRAPHY

Bailey, Kenneth E. *Poet & Peasant*. Grand Rapids: Eerdmans, 1976.

———. *Through Peasant Eyes: A Literary-Cultural Approach to the Parables in Luke*. Grand Rapids: Eerdmans, 1980.

Blomberg, Craig L. *Interpreting the Parables*. Downers Grove: InterVarsity, 1990.

Borsch, Frederick Houk. *Many Things in Parables: Extravagant Stories of the New Community*. Philadelphia: Fortress, 1988.

Carson, Donald A. *Matthew*. Expositor's Bible Commentary. Grand Rapids: Zondervan, 1982.

Craddock, Fred B. *Luke*. Interpretation: A Bible Commentary for Teaching and Preaching. Louisville: John Knox Press, 1990.

Fee, Gordon D., and Douglas Stuart. *How To Read the Bible for All Its Worth*. 2nd Ed. Grand Rapids: Zondervan, 1993.

Hultgren, Arland J. *The Parables of Jesus: a Commentary*. Grand Rapids: Eerdmans, 2000.

Jordan, Clarence. *The Cotton Patch Version of Luke and Acts: Jesus' Doings and the Happenings*. New York: A Koinonia Publication, 1969.

Kistemaker, Simon J. *The Parables: Understanding the Stories Jesus Told*. Grand Rapids: Baker, 1980.

McArthur, Harvey K., and Robert M. Johnston. *They Also Taught in Parables: Rabbinic Parables from the First Centuries of the Christian Era*. Grand Rapids: Zondervan, 1990.

Scott, Bernard Brandon. *Hear Then the Parable: A Commentary on the Parables of Jesus*. Minneapolis: Fortress, 1989.

Vallet, Ronald E. *Stepping Stones of the Steward*. 2nd Ed. Grand Rapids: Eerdmans, 1994.

Walvoord, John F. *Matthew: Thy Kingdom Come*. Chicago: Moody, 1974.

Young, Brad H. *The Parables: Jewish Tradition and Christian Interpretation*. Peabody, MA: Hendrickson, 1998.

INDEX OF PARABLES

INDEX OF SCRIPTURES

INDEX OF SCRIPTURES (con't)

INDEX OF SCRIPTURES (con't)

INDEX OF WORDS

INDEX OF WORDS (con't)

Printed in the United States
51445LVS00005B/337-357